Jeremiah 29:11: "For I know the plans I have for you," declares the Lord, "plans to prosper you and not to harm you, plans to give you hope and a future."

DO YOU SIT AROUND AND WONDER: WHAT IS MY PURPOSE IN LIFE?

DO YOU WONDER WHY IT FEELS AS IF YOU GO THROUGH SO MUCH?

God has placed us on earth for a purpose greater than we could ever imagine. Life seems to be unfair sometimes when you only focus on the obstacles, trials, scars, and bad times you have been through. However, God has equipped you with everything you need. God has a way of teaching you lessons and building your character, strength, and faith in Him through what appear to be obstacles, trials, scars, and bad times. You have to look at these situations as purposeful and intentional, not as bad things. Reflect on all that Jesus had to experience while He was here on earth to fulfill God's plan for His life. The purpose Jesus completed while being here required more suffering than you endure, yet you complain. Ask yourself why? God is intentional and everything you experience is for a greater purpose. We have the power of freewill so we can make whatever decisions we want. God gives us that opportunity. He does not make us believe in Him, and He surely does not make us walk in His will. We decide what we want to choose.

This small, dynamic, and insightful book teaches people that everyone is PREGNANT WITH A PURPOSE *and that your* SCARS CHRIST ALLOWED TO RESCUE SOMEONE. *In this book, the author shares some of her powerful testimony and guides you through the process of finding your purpose in God by explaining the importance of why you must:* EXPERIENCE SCARS IN LIFE TO PREPARE YOU FOR YOUR PURPOSE IN GOD, BUILD A CONTINUOUS RELATIONSHIP WITH GOD, EXERCISE YOUR FAITH IN GOD DAILY, CRY OUT TO GOD CONTINUOUSLY, ASK GOD WHAT YOUR PURPOSE IS, BE OPEN AND WILLING TO GO THROUGH THE PROCESS OF DELIVERANCE. AND MUCH MORE!

PREGNANT WITH A PURPOSE

Scars Christ Allowed to Rescue Someone

PREGNANT WITH A PURPOSE

Scars Christ Allowed to Rescue Someone

Taneisha L. Naylor

Pregnant with a Purpose: Scars Christ Allowed to Rescue Someone
Copyright ©2016 Taneisha L Naylor

MacKenzie Publishing
Halifax, Nova Scotia

ISBN-13: 978-1927529416
ISBN-10: 1927529417
December 2016

Cover Artist: James Ryan

Edited by: C.A. MacKenzie

ഹൽൽ
MacKenzie Publishing

Dedication

I dedicate this book to God and to my precious daughter, Royalty.

God, all of my life you have been by my side. I never understood all I went through until I started to seek you wholeheartedly. It wasn't until I completely surrendered and submitted to you that I clearly understood my purpose in life. Thank you for showing me that you have created everyone on earth with purposes deep down in our womb and that it's up to us to seek you and discover our purpose. God, thank you for all the scars you allowed me to endure through life, which ultimately allowed me to give birth to this book and my purpose.

Royalty, you changed my life and confirmed even more my purpose. Thank you for walking this journey of blind faith with me and God. Thank you for allowing God to use you in my life. I love you forever, and I am thankful that God choose me to be your mother.

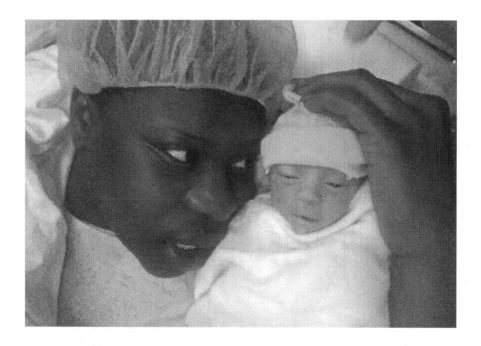

Acknowledgments

First off, I thank God for everything He has done in my life. For every scar, trial, tribulation, and obstacle. I thank Him for restoration, healing, love, joy, peace, clarity, confirmation; for my family, friends, and enemies. I thank God for allowing me to write this book. I thank God for giving me revelation that all of His children are Pregnant With A Purpose in life.

I thank God for allowing me to be a mother. I thank God for my powerful blessing, Royalty. I am thankful to God for my mother, my father, and all my siblings who I love so dearly.

I thank God for my lovely sister from another mother, Monique Rodgers. She was my rock while on this journey with Royalty and continues to be.

I am thankful for the powerful Celeste Davis and her wonderful children. They have been here for me during the hardest times in my life.

I thank Felicia Fewell for her encouragement, wisdom, and love to help me write this book. I thank God for Paul and Danielle Harris for always being there for encouragement, wisdom, and spiritual guidance going through this season of my life. I thank God for Richard Taylor stepping right in, connecting me with the right resources, giving me wisdom and encouragement to get through the ending portion of my book. I am thankful to God for bringing everyone together to help me create this masterpiece.

I thank Catherine A. MacKenzie for allowing God to use her in my life and for being so patient, kind, loving, and understanding as I finished this book. I acknowledge her amazing work, and without her I don't know what I would have done.

Table of Contents

Introduction

I've always been spiritual. When I was a child, people were amazed with the words that came from my mouth. As I matured and desired to know God on a deeper level, I knew I had to read more of the Bible and pray more often.

During my search, I learned so much about myself. God opened up my eyes to things I had said as a child. He let me know the words were not from me but from the Holy Spirit, and He showed me that certain things I used to say were in the Bible. Back then, of course, I had no idea that anything I said was Biblical. It's funny how God uses children to spread His wisdom and glory.

In my search to know God deeper, I began to see Him in a whole new light. My spiritual relationship with God grew through prayer, worship, and the reading of scriptures. God revealed to me how He created us all in His image. Those characteristics of God are the same characteristics that are deeply embedded in us. God showed me how He truly lives in me and confirmed how He is always and forever with us. God showed me that everything I have been through is for a reason.

Each year, I grew more in Christ and was able to see that God was all I ever needed, wanted, and desired. God created me and knows the depths of my soul. God is powerful and truly amazing in all His ways. I had to grow and learn that God does not make mistakes and is not a coincidental God. He is intentional.

Growing up, I was always misunderstood by family and friends. I was the oddball. My family used to say: "She always got something to say," and "She think she know everything." They used both of these phrases in negative and positive connotations, more negatively than positively. When they wanted to know something, they would say, "Go ask 411." When they were upset at me for having a different thought than they did, they'd say, "She think she know everything."

The more I grew in Christ and the more knowledge I was given, the more of an outcast I became. Despite that, I still had confidence even when people tried to tear down my self-esteem. Growing up I had more wisdom and knowledge than most of my peers. I would look at my friends, family, and others around me and try to make better decisions than they did. I always desired to have a greater future and most people around me did not seem to make decisions that led them to a greater future.

If I saw friends or family make mistakes and the consequences that followed, I'd try to think of a better decision so I wouldn't get the same outcome. Now, don't get me wrong; I wasn't perfect and not always on point. I've struggled with such things as self-esteem, confidence, decision-making, faith, and obedience.

However, I've always had confidence in God. I've always had confidence in my sense of decision-making. I've always had confidence in my abilities, gifts, and talents. I knew He was always there with me, and I learned at a young age if God put me through something, it was for a reason. I never quite knew the reason, but I had confidence and joy knowing that it was God and that His plan was far greater than my own.

As a youngster, I was never really afraid of much. My mom said I used to wave at people, give hugs, and say hello everywhere we went. She said I was always smiling and happy and that I never met a stranger. Now, when I say I wasn't afraid, I speak about things that most kids would be afraid of. I was outspoken at a young age as well. I always said how I felt and always desired to share the wisdom and knowledge I was given. I also loved to encourage and motivate people at a young age.

However, throughout life, Satan has sent so many demons on assignments to kill, steal, and destroy everything that God has given me: purpose, self-worth, self-esteem, health, family, peace of mind, gifts, abilities, talents, relationships. I've always known the devil was real. I just had little knowledge of the devil and his tactics while growing up. I always knew he was an "opp," meaning the devil was our opponent.

I knew the devil was not here for our good and that he was against the plan of God, but I had no idea how to fight against the tricks, tactics, and gimmicks of Satan. As I've grown, I learned more about Satan through sermons preached by pastors, reading the Bible, and revelation from God. I learned more about Satan's plans, tactics, and assignments. I learned how to identify the devil and the power of rebuking him, but for some reason he continued to come back with the same tricks, using different people, different days, and different years.

One thing I learned about the devil was that he's smart. Sometimes we think we are getting a blessing from God, but it can be a curse from the devil. This is a trick we fall for when our foundation is weak. If we do not truly know God and if we do not truly know of Satan's history, we can fall for Satan's tricks. We have to be able to determine the difference between tests from God and tricks from Satan.

During my pregnancy with my baby girl, Royalty Sarai Jones, God revealed so much to me. He showed me my purpose and Royalty's purpose. He showed me how powerful He created me to be, how to forgive others, how to forgive myself, and how to forgive Him. He showed me the process of healing, and so much more. God gave me an abundant amount of strength, peace, joy, love, and wisdom that I did not understand. Nor did I understand the people around me.

God did not show me everything I would have wanted Him to show me during my pregnancy, but He revealed other things after I gave birth. God also revealed things to me little by little during the writing of this book. Sometimes we ask God to show us the reason for everything we are going through all at once, but God knows what we can handle and when we can handle it, so God will reveal things piece-by-piece as needed.

After the birth of my precious baby girl, God showed me how powerful I was with Him and the importance to live by His will instead of my own. He revealed curses that were spoken over my life by myself and others; the demons that have been attached and assigned to me and how to cast them out. He took me through the process of healing and deliverance that for years I had cried out for. I learned and experienced deliverance on a whole new level. He gave me spiritual eyes like never before. He showed me how disobedience comes with curses from God. I specify this because we think that every scar or obstacle is from Satan. The Book of Deuteronomy teaches that God blesses us through our obedience and curses us through our disobedience.

This book was birthed through this process of healing and deliverance. God had already predestined me to write books. I just did not know exactly when. Three years ago, I went through the process of starting and never finishing writing a book because it was not in God's timing. I learned if it is God's timing, then nothing can stop it. No demon in hell can stop what God wants.

Royalty truly came and fulfilled her purpose. God instructed me throughout my pregnancy to share my story. He instructed that I use social media as an outlet to testify and allow people to witness my walk with Christ. I shared my story little by little, all along giving God the Glory. The devil was pissed with me and my obedience to God during this process. A massive number of people shared with me how moved they were by my walk with God during this time.

People commented on my posts, sent me direct messages, and told me when they saw my posts how much of a blessing it was to watch my journey with Royalty. Some people told me I encouraged them to form a relationship with God, to trust Him, to pray more, to read the word more, and to be obedient to Him. People expressed how they admired my strength and how they would have been given up. I always replied, "But God…" and "To God be the glory."

During this season, God confirmed my purpose like never before. God made it plain and simple what my purpose had been since I was in my mother's womb. Through it all, I've grown to trust God in all His ways and to walk blindly in faith. Faith is believing in things unseen. Faith is knowing God is always with you. Faith is letting God lead the way. Faith is being obedient and patient with God. Faith is following God's will versus your will. Faith is loving God during the good and the bad times. Faith is crying out to God, praying, reading the word, and still pressing when you don't see any change. Faith is running after God, surrendering, and submitting completely to God. Once you do this, you will see God manifest things in your life you have dreamed of and some things you never imagined.

My encouragement to you is to try God for yourself. As you read my book, I talk about pieces of my journey, revelations from God, instructions on how to build a foundation with God, and wisdom that God has given me to share with others. This is only a small, watered-down version of my full testimony. However, it is profound because it reveals how my purpose was confirmed and the demons I had to identify and fight against. It shows the power of God and the beauty of God and His predestination for our lives. I pray you are blessed by this book and can take away what God wants you to take away.

Every day before you read this book, pray. A prayer follows should you not know what to say.

Prayer

Lord, thank you for waking me up today

Thank you for being such a great God

Thank you for loving me when I don't love myself

Lord, thank you for my family, friends, and enemies

Lord God, continue to protect us from things seen and unseen

Lord, send legions of angels around us each day

God, as I read this book, send me revelation, instruction, and wisdom that I need to get through

Show me why I am reading this book

Begin to open up wells in me that I have not noticed

Begin to clean all the dirt, clutter, and mess out of my mind, heart, and spirit

God, make me clean. Make me new, make me whole

God, lead me where you want me to go, guide me, cover me with the blood of Jesus

God, show me you in ways that I have never seen

God, send me all the fruits of the spirit

Lord, save me, heal me, deliver me

God, I love you and I believe in you

Take everything away from me that I don't need

God, begin to give me spiritual eyes like never before and show me what I need to see

Give me wisdom, knowledge, discernment, and understanding that I have never had

God, begin to reveal my purpose to me and show me why I have been through all that I have been through

Lord God, I want people to see your light shining from me

I want people to see you and hear you when they see and hear me

God, use me

God, allow me to speak words that are only from you

Lord God, increase my faith

Lord, I trust you

I trust you, Lord

I love you and I thank you

Amen.

Scriptures

[3] Blessed are the poor in spirit, for theirs is the kingdom of heaven. [4] Blessed are those who mourn, for they will be comforted. [5] Blessed are the meek, for they will inherit the earth. [6] Blessed are those who hunger and thirst for righteousness, for they will be filled. [7] Blessed are the merciful, for they will be shown mercy. [8] Blessed are the pure in heart, for they will see God. [9] Blessed are the peacemakers, for they will be called children of God. [10] Blessed are those who are persecuted because of righteousness, for theirs is the kingdom of heaven. [11] Blessed are you when people insult you, persecute you and falsely say all kinds of evil against you because of me. [Matthew 5:3-11]

[14] You are the light of the world. A town built on a hill cannot be hidden. [15] Neither do people light a lamp and put it under a bowl. Instead they put it on its stand, and it gives light to everyone in the house. [16] In the same way, let your light shine before others, that they may see your good deeds and glorify your Father in heaven. [Matthew 5:14-16]

Chapter 1

Scars

When you see scars, what do you think about? I think of bruises, cuts, scrapes, pain, hurt, sadness, madness, and anger.

The Google definitions for Scar:

- *a mark left on the skin or within body tissue where a wound, burn, or sore has not healed completely and fibrous connective tissue has developed.*

- *a lasting effect of grief, fear, or other emotion left on a person's character by a traumatic experience.*

- *Synonyms are other words that can be used to explain or replace the word. The synonyms for scar are mark, blemish, disfigurement, discoloration and defacement.*

I wrote this book to address the scars that we have been given. As a child, when you were hurt or bruised, you were taught it was okay to cry, and then they gave you a bandage to cover it up. In my adult years, I learned that a bandage was there to stop the bleeding and cover up the bruise or scar. A bandage is not used to heal the scar or bruise. The body heals on its own during a process.

As a child, I picked at my scars while they were healing, so they left marks on my skin. My mother always told me not to pick at them. Now that I'm older, I see scars on my body from when I was younger. The wounds have healed over time, leaving indentations on my skin to remind me of the afflictions I experienced.

That is how scars to our spirit work as well. From the time we are born until the time we die, we experience scars of our spiritual, mental, physical, and emotional well-being. All of us were created in our own uniquely special way by God, with assignments and purposes. We also were predestined to go through our storms, trials, and obstacles. These storms, trials, and obstacles sometimes leave scars and afflictions on our bodies and/or in our hearts.

I have grown to learn that everything you have been through was designed for you to fulfill your purpose. Now, the thing I love most about God is that we have the ability to make our own decisions. I believe that is the greatest thing He has given us as humans, but this can also be the most destructive thing as well. Sometimes we make a decision that we know is not good for our spiritual, emotional, physical, or emotional well-being. And sometimes God allows it to happen, meaning He has the power to stop anything but allows us to experience situations for our growth, to test our faith, to bring us closer to Him, and all along to bring glory to His name.

In 2014, I came across a book called *F.R.E.E.* (Finally Realizing Experiences for Expansion) in which the author broke down each letter into a chapter. She guided the reader through each chapter in order to dig into your memory bank and meditate on your journey through life. Her message was to get you to the point to finally realize the experiences you have been through were purposed before God expanded you. This book was deep and allowed me to grow. I was able to look at all my experiences—good and bad—and rejoice knowing that God was with me all along and that His plans were greater than my own.

During that same time, I met the author of this book because she offered me a free Life Coaching class. I eventually paid for another session with her, which included an hour with her and a copy of her book.

Now, God is an intentional God and pre-planned our lives before our birth. God already knew he would send that woman to me in my time of need. He had purposed her to write her book, and her book and coaching would bless and shift me spiritually, mentally, and emotionally. God is a great God. We may not understand why things happen when they do, but once you are in a place where you are seeking and trusting God, He will reveal to you why things happen as they do.

Our lives were created for God's greater plan, which no one on Earth knows. Only God knows. Our jobs are to follow God, submit, surrender, and trust Him in all of His ways and thoughts. Isaiah 55:8 states: "'For my thoughts are not your thoughts, neither are your ways my ways,' declares the LORD." We do not need to overthink God's plan for our lives. We don't need to stop trusting God because He did not bless us with something we wanted. God knows what is best and what is not. God knows you far better than you know yourself. Some things you think you can handle, but God knows you can't. You may not be able to handle the consequences that come along with it.

It is okay to come to God and ask Him for wisdom and understanding. But are you ready for the revelations from God? Also, something that brings me great joy and allows me to rejoice in the midst of a storm is knowing that God has allowed this test. The trials you go through are not because God does not love you. The devil will try to get into your mind and into a dark place mentally and try to speak everything opposite of God. That is why the devil is an opp. He is not for you, and you have to remember the devil's plans and God's plans for your lives are different.

The thief comes only to steal and kill and destroy; I have come that they may have life, and have it to the full. [John 10:10 NIV]

This scripture confirms to you and clearly states the plans of God and the devil. The devil wants to make you believe the opposite of what God wants you to believe. The devil wants to have your mind. If God does not have your mind, the devil must have it. Anything or anyone that is not God is an idol. An idol is something you give your mind, heart, thoughts, and time to. Idols are used as scapegoats from the devil. He has ways of tricking you to think that you are not worshipping and believing in Him but someone or something else. Remember, if it is not of God, it is of the devil.

God specifically told us many times in the Bible not to worship other gods and not to have any idols.

You shall not worship their gods, nor serve them, nor do according to their deeds; but you shall utterly overthrow them and break their sacred pillars in pieces. [Exodus 23:24]

You shall not make for yourself an idol, or any likeness of what is in heaven above or on the earth beneath or in the water under the earth. [Deuteronomy 5:8]

God also forewarned us many times in the Bible about the consequences to worshipping other gods and idols.

And my eye will not spare, nor will I have pity. I will punish you according to your ways, while your abominations are in your midst. Then you will know that I am the LORD, who strikes. [Ezekiel 7:9 ESV]

You will be fully repaid for all your prostitution--your worship of idols. Yes, you will suffer the full penalty. Then you will know that I am the Sovereign LORD. [Ezekiel 23:49 NLT]

Some of our own scars are caused by us. Remember that God is still God and that no weapon formed against you shall prosper. At this point, I encourage you to journal through the course of reading this book. First, start by digging deep into your memory bank and writing down things that have scarred you over the years that you can't seem to forget, things that still control you, things that you feel you will never forget, things that made you feel as if God did not love you because you went through it, mistakes that you may have made and consequences that followed. After you finish, pray and talk to God. Ask God to reveal things to you that you have buried and suppressed. Tell God you want to be clean and made whole.

As you are writing and talking to God, ask Him to give you revelation and understanding as to why He allowed those very things to happen. Ask God to show you your purpose. God is a prayer answering God. As you pray, believe that God will answer your prayers and give you answers and understanding. God gives you what you need at the time. Not everything you want is given to you at once. You may be in a season of teaching from God. He may not be ready to reveal completely to you your purpose. There are probably still experiences you have to go through before He reveals your purpose to you completely.

I pray that your search and seek with God is everything you want it to be and more. God is going to show you His miraculous powers during this time. I am excited you are picking up this book and taking this journey to find your purpose. I know God will reveal it to you in the season He predestined to reveal it to you. He is sharpening and tightening every broken, chipped, bitter, and loose end. Get ready for the shifting of God in your life.

In this time of your seek, it is important you read the word, pray, worship, and have quiet time with God daily. As time progresses, your time spent with God needs to increase. You need to hear from God at all times. You need to talk to God all the time. God needs to be able to reach you at all times. My encouragement to you is to get in a Christian-based church that preaches from the Bible. I highly encourage, eventually, a deliverance ministry to become involved with. Also, find spiritual friends who are on a deeper level than you are. Connect with people. Network and exchange contacts. Tell them where you are currently and where you want to be. Do not be afraid, because in this season it is crucial and you need spiritual warriors around you.

If you get off track, don't run from God. Start over again. God is not through with you. God is not mad at you. God is more concerned with your heart and your progress, not where you are. The beauty of God is that He meets us where we are. Get ready for what God has in store for you.

Be blessed while reading this book. My prayer is that you understand why God has allowed scars in your life and that through this process God reveals your purpose as He did for me.

I will share parts of my story and tests I have been through that many of you can relate to. I will share my journey of being pregnant with a purpose and how deliverance is important in the process. Buckle your seatbelts, and get ready for this ride you are about to experience. I love you.

God's way is perfect. All the lord's promises prove true. He is a shield for all who look to him for protection. [Psalm 18:30]

Chapter 2

The Cry Out to God

Have you ever been in a place so broken where you didn't know where to go or what to do next? Have you ever felt alone, as if no one was there for you? Have you ever felt as though no one truly understood you and where you were in life? Have you ever been hungry and thirsty for God? Have you ever needed God to save you, heal you, comfort you, protect you, love you, give you peace, joy, understanding, wisdom, money, and just more of Him? Have you ever broken down, got on your knees, and cried out to God? Have you ever sat in your car, in your house, or at work and cried out to God, "I NEED YOU, LORD. I NEED YOUR PRESENCE, OH GOD. FIGHT FOR ME, GOD. LIGHT THE WAY, GOD. I'M LOST. I'M BROKEN. I'M CONFUSED. I NEED YOU, OH GOD?"

I'm sure I'm not alone, and I'm sure many of you reading this book are at that place in life right now or have been at some point. In this place, you are literally stuck, lost, confused, hurt, broken, and ashamed. Fear and doubt also show up and manifest.

In December of 2015, I was twelve weeks pregnant with Royalty. At my very first visit to the doctor, I received a fatal diagnosis for my baby. I did not know what the diagnosis truly meant and where I was going, but I immediately remembered that God was with me and had control of it. The doctor said something profound and needed in the moment. He said, "There is nothing that you did to cause this. There is nothing that you can do to change this, and there is nothing that we can do to change this. This is a rare disease, and we don't know much about it. There is very little research about this disease."

Those words were spoken directly from God. God just used the doctor, who probably had no idea he was being used. I have learned that many times God uses people to deliver His message and sometimes the people delivering the message are unaware at the time that God is using them.

When I received this news, I knew God was with me and felt His presence. I'm not saying I wasn't sad, hurt, and broken, because I was. But not for one second did I question God and ask, "Why me and my baby?" I just trusted Him. I was at the point in life where I had learned time and time again that God is in control no matter what.

A few days prior to my first visit to the doctor, I went to the emergency room. The doctors expressed their concerns about water in my baby's brain. They didn't give many details but suggested I go to a specialist as soon as possible. After returning home that night, knowing something was wrong, I broke down. My relationship with Brian, the child's father, was failing, and there was so much tension, animosity, and built-up pain that we took it out on each other. We were in unhealthy places mentally, emotionally, physically, and spiritually. I don't believe that either of us knew then what we were dealing with.

I didn't see the full picture until God allowed me to take a few steps back to look at the situation from a different angle. I pretended I had everything under control and that everything I dealt with was due to the pregnancy, but deep inside, old issues I had not dealt with were preventing me to live the way God wanted me to. I tried to talk to friends, family, the child's father, and mentors about my feelings, looking for a magical answer and solution to my problems, but no one had an answer. I also talked to these people for comfort at the time, not realizing exactly what I was doing.

When I sat back and talked to God, more and more things changed. I asked God so many questions regarding my situation: God, what are you going to do? God, can you heal my baby? God, what do I need to do? God, what does this mean? God, will you heal my baby? God, can you fix this relationship? I asked God so many questions, and each day I had a new question. I soon cried out to God every day because I wanted God to suddenly perform miracles in my baby's life and my own.

God revealed things to me and gave me instructions on what to do, but I still felt stuck. He was not telling me what I wanted to hear, but definitely what I needed to hear. He had to put me in such a place so I could seek Him more, hear Him, cry out to Him, and get my life right with Him. I had been neglecting Him during my pregnancy. I had tried my hardest to live a life I desired, but I was not including Him as I needed to. I thought I was in control, but I wasn't, so He had to show me that He—God—was in control. His ways and His will for my life is far greater than my ways and my will for my life.

God made many things clearer as I cried out to Him, including how I held onto people past their expiration date. God showed me that if I kept doing what I wanted to do that I would always stay in the same place. In that place, I was broken, confused, frustrated, hurt, tired, pained, angry, and unhappy. I felt unloved and that I lived a lie and wasn't fulfilling my purpose.

I cried out to God and asked Him what I needed to do. I asked the Lord to change my life, my mind, my heart, my soul, and my surroundings. I told Him I wanted the life He had for me and that I was tired of trying to do things on my own. I told Him I knew I had messed up and that I was sorry. I repented. I also told God I didn't know how to get out of what I was experiencing.

God told me my situation was predestined by him and that I had no control over it. God told me to trust the process, to not rush the process, and to stay the process. God told me He needed me to be where I was and that He had things for me to do in this season. God told me if He had not taken me through the wilderness, He would not have been able to get me to cry out to Him, seek Him, and reach the place of surrendering to Him.

Throughout life, while I was going through my trials, tests, and obstacles, there were times I did not trust God like I needed to and times I did not trust Him at all. Sometimes I doubted God and His abilities. There were times I thought I could control or figure out a situation on my own. Then there were times when I doubted myself and what I was capable of. Many times I did not seek Him before making a decision and did what I wanted to do. Now that I look back over my life, I can honestly say that I put more trust in me than I did in God. I verbally said I trusted Him, but my actions did not always show that.

Then God revealed to me on a deeper level that I needed Him and only Him. I needed to trust Him and only Him, and I needed to surrender to Him and only Him. So, I cried out to Him. He heard my cry and eventually answered. Everything in me began to change, but everything did not happen immediately.

The righteous cry out, and the LORD hears them; he delivers them from all their troubles. **[Psalms 34:17]**

Chapter 3

Don't Worry About the How,

When, and Why

God said, "Write the vision and make it plain on tablets, that he may run who reads it." [Habakuk 2:2]

This scripture is powerful to me, as are other scriptures in the Bible. However, I picked it for the purpose of explaining a few points. First, God will give us a vision and, over time, show us glimpses of this vision. It is up to us to believe that the vision is possible with God. Many things and people will try to distract, detour, and deny you of your God-given vision. That is why it's so important to be obedient to God and put one hundred percent of your faith in God, and God alone. The key to activating anything in life is to believe in God.

In the scripture above, God makes it plain and gives us exact instructions on what to do when He gives us a vision. Write it down. Why is it so hard for us as humans to follow instructions from God? It does not matter if the instructions come from a scripture, a book, a manual, an individual, or God talking directly to us. Is it that we try to tell ourselves we don't know the voice of God? Or is it that we are

22

afraid, doubt, lack faith, and overall ignore the provisions God has given us?

I dare you to seek God more through prayer and in reading the Bible. I dare you to call on God, ask Him for guidance, and ask Him for things in prayer. I dare you to listen to God when He gives you directions. I dare you to believe that God answers your prayers. I dare you to allow Him to lead you. I dare you to trust Him in everything you do. I dare you to follow Him and see where He takes you. I dare you to thank God for all He does for you. I dare you to praise God in advance for the things you believe He will do. I dare you to worship God in public and in private. I dare you to love God on a level that you never have before. I dare you to put God first. I dare you to put your plans away and ask God what His plans are for your life.

A few years ago, God told me I would be an author of many books and that He would use me to bring people nearer to Him by sharing my struggles while giving Him the glory. I was somewhat shocked but excited at the same time. I was more than thankful, but immediately I thought, **How** *would this be possible?* I focused on my current situation and became completely distracted.

When I was younger, I always felt life was hard. I had been through stuff, but I never thought I would write a book about it. Hearing this revelation from God was funny, strange, and great all at the same time. As the years passed, life got much harder, but God used me to share pieces of my story and encourage others along the way. However, at the start of the sharing of my story, I was unaware of How and Why God was using me. Once I realized I was allowing God to use me, I still never thought I would write a book. After sharing my story often and individuals telling me I was helpful and encouraging, I realized I had a story to tell.

I've always loved to encourage, build, educate, and uplift people. I was still confused, asking God multiple questions, such as "**How** are you going to use me?" God told me not to worry about **how**, **why**, and **when** but to remember that He is always with me. God also whispered to me, "There are still things I need you to go through first before you write the book."

I said okay to His will and His way. I bought journals and wrote to God. I researched how to write books. I read books to expand my mind. I talked to God more often and read the Bible more. I would have seasons where I would write all the time and seasons where I did not journal at all.

The Holy Spirit then instructed me to reach people through social media, so I started to use Facebook and Instagram as tools to write statuses to encourage and educate the masses while giving God the glory. People commented on my Facebook to thank me for the scriptures, encouraging words, and testimonies. I received a lot of Facebook messages from people telling me I encouraged them to find God and/or to rebuild their relationship with Him. People also sent me messages asking me to pray for them or asking for instructions on how to pray.

I was astounded by the response I received, but then I remembered all the things God had told me. God told me he would use me to bring people nearer to Him and that I would be an author of many books.

He also told me I would have a nonprofit company and that I would focus on the underprivileged and at-risk youth. He informed me that my organization would grow and that He would provide me with a building and employees to help fulfill this vision. He revealed many other assignments, as well, for which He created me. I was elated once again but immediately wondered **how, why me, when, who,** and **what.**

At that moment, even though I had a lot of questions for God, I believed Him. I truly did. I believed in that very moment that God could change my situation and use me for His glory just as He told me. He was already using me and had been all my life. Even before I recognized God's hand over my life, my gifts, and my purposes, he was using me.

While God gave me visions, I focused on the **how,** and in that moment I realized that wondering **how** blocked me from receiving blessings from God. God does not want us to worry about the **how, why, when,** and the behind-the-scenes work. He wants us to be obedient, follow Him, and trust Him so that He can do His will in our lives. This is all done in the process of trusting God for the things you do not see and imagining how it will happen. This process is called exercising your faith.

God wants you to know the realities of experiencing Him, which I found in the book *Experiencing God* by Claude King, Henry and Richard Blackaby:

- God is always at work around you.
- God pursues a continued love relationship with you that is real.

- God invites you to become involved with Him and His work.
- God speaks through the Holy Spirit, the Bible, prayer, through circumstances, and the church to reveal Himself to you.
- God invites you to work with Him.
- God wants you to make major adjustments in your life to join Him with what He is doing.

You come to know God by experience as you obey Him. So, as you continue to read this book, I pray that you are drawn closer to God. I pray that you allow God to use you in whatever way He is trying to use you. I encourage you to walk out on faith and to exercise your faith daily. Remember that God is ALWAYS with you, guiding you, instructing you, and He lives in you. God created us all in His image. No one is greater than you. Lean on God and trust Him during the good and the bad. God's plan and His will for our lives are far greater than our own. I pray that you can trust in God with all your heart. I pray that what I have opened up to share in these pages blesses you, encourages you, and strengthens you. You are not alone.

I wrote this book because God gave me instructions, willpower, strength, courage, and power. I encourage you to listen to God's voice and allow Him to lead you. I encourage you today to share a part of your story with someone because you never know who you can help.

Remember, you are never alone and you can do ANYTHING you put your mind to.

I can do all things through Christ who strengthens me. [Philippians 4:13]

Chapter 4

Exercise Your Faith

God has dealt to every man a measure of faith. It is up to us to exercise our faith. Some of us dream to be healthier, fitter, and stronger, so we buy a membership to the gym. We plan to work out, eat healthier, build muscle, and lose weight. Our goal and hopes are to lose weight, look better, and become healthier as time progresses. We usually set a target date with a target weight to reach. We hope and pray that we accomplish the goal that we envisioned at the start.

In order to achieve this goal, you must be consistent in working out and eating healthier. You have to wait for results, as they come over time. The results can sometimes take a long time before you actually see them because you are training your mind and body to do something new. As you see small results, you become happier and more enthused to work out. You obtain a different talk and walk, and you feel and look like a new person. Then, BAM! You reach the goal and vision you had set.

Over the days of going to the gym and changing old habits, you were building character, strength, perseverance, and a new testimony. You did not know at the beginning that you were doing all these things, because your goal was to look better and be healthier. Ultimately, you became a better person, and you learned much about yourself and God throughout this process.

This is exactly how exercising your faith works. You have to work that thang out daily. You have to continuously exercise that thang even when you feel weak and are in pain and don't see any results. Achievement seems so far away, but you have to remain focused and keep God first. The more you exercise your faith, the more it grows; the more you trust God, the more you allow God to lead you without the fear of the unknown. Trusting God brings peace and joy. I can assure you that God will lead you, but will you follow?

God will show His love for you, but do you believe Him? God will show you glimpses of places He will take you. Do you trust Him? God wakes you up every morning. Do you trust him to do that? Or are you like some people who think if you set an alarm clock, the alarm will wake you? I hope you don't think like that. God wakes you, feeds you, put clothes on your back, and blesses you daily. Do you trust him every day to do all these things?

I sure do, and it gives me joy and peace knowing I have a God who will supply all my needs. I can attest to the fact that I've been in positions where I did not fully have trust in God and did not believe in Him for all things. I am thankful God changed my thoughts, ways, and actions. God has put me in seasons that would have most people stop believing there is a God. In these seasons, God showed me truly who He is and always will be. God is a way maker, provider, healer, deliverer, and so much more.

During the period in which I was new to exercising my faith and building a closer relationship with God, I craved to know more about Him. I did not want to simply believe or know Him from what others told me about Him. I did not want to simply believe what I heard at church and from online sermons. I desired to know and trust God deeper. Through this time, God always lead me to whom and what I needed to hear, read, and/or witness. I came across so many scriptures that brought insight, wisdom, joy, peace, understanding, direction, and healing to my heart. It showed me who God truly was, still is, and will be, and His power.

Here are a few scriptures I love that helped me exercise my faith.

25 Therefore I tell you, do not worry about your life, what you will eat or drink; or about your body, what you will wear. Is not life more than food, and the body more than clothes? 26 Look at the birds of the air; they do not sow or reap or store away in barns, and yet your heavenly Father feeds them. Are you not much more valuable than they? 27 Can any one of you by worrying add a single hour to your life? 28 And why do you worry about clothes? See how the flowers of the field grow. They do not labor or spin. 29 Yet I tell you that not even Solomon in all his splendor was dressed like one of these. 30 If that is how God clothes the grass of the field, which is here today and tomorrow is thrown into the fire, will he not much more clothe you—you of little faith? 31 So do not worry, saying, "What shall we eat?" or "What shall we drink?" or "What shall we wear?" 32 For the pagans run after all these things, and your heavenly Father knows that you need them. ³³ But seek first his kingdom and his righteousness, and all these things will be given to you as well. ³⁴ Therefore do not worry about tomorrow, for tomorrow will worry about itself. Each day has enough trouble of its own. [Matthew 6:25-34 (NIV)]

The foregoing is one of my favorite scriptures that continues to remind me who God is and not to worry about anything. Verse 34 says enough in itself. It reminds me to rest in God and worry about nothing.

Trust in the Lord with all your heart and lean not on your own understanding... [Proverbs 3:5]

And without faith it is impossible to please God, because anyone who comes to him must believe that he exists and that he rewards those who earnestly seek him. [Hebrews 11:6]

For we also have had the good news proclaimed to us, just as they did; but the message they heard was of no value to them, because they did not share the faith of those who obeyed. 3 Now we who have believed enter that rest, just as God has said... [Hebrews 4:2-3]

In God, whose word I praise—in God I trust and am not afraid. What can mere mortals do to me? [Psalm 56: 4]

²³ Then he got into the boat and his disciples followed him. ²⁴ Suddenly a furious storm came up on the lake, so that the waves swept over the boat. But Jesus was sleeping. ²⁵ The disciples went and woke him, saying, "Lord, save us! We're going to drown!" ²⁶ He replied, "You of little faith, why are you so afraid?" Then he

got up and rebuked the winds and the waves, and it was completely calm. ²⁷ The men were amazed and asked, "What kind of man is this? Even the winds and the waves obey him!"
[Matthew 8:23-27]

The foregoing scriptures are very powerful to me and show us how powerful and mighty God is. If we trust in Him, we can be just as powerful and mighty. Continuously, we learn as we grow in life and seek God. When our faith is tested, He wants to see if we believe in Him. God wants to know whether you have faith in Him like you tell others or if you simply have faith in yourself and man. During the trials of life that test our faith, God is stretching us and building us for where He is getting ready to take us. Remember, there will never be a testimony without a test. Always keep in mind that the enemy would not be working so hard to attack you if he did not already know there is a greater testimony to give that you are not even aware of.

The enemy is here to kill, steal, and destroy. He begs and pleads with God, asking God for permission to attack you. Yes, I said he asks God for permission. The enemy has no dominion, power, or authority over your life. God has to give him permission to attack you. Do not get discouraged or lose faith when trials and obstacles are present. You would not have any opposition if you were not highly favored from God. I have learned over time to be thankful when I face trials because God is preparing me for something better.

There have been times in my life when things were all good, yet I prayed for a storm because I knew after the storm came the rain and after the rain, the sunshine. It is a must for God to shake things up in our lives so that He can teach us lessons before He blesses us. He has to show us that He is always present: guiding us, equipping us, fighting for us, leading us; He is continually blessing us even in the storm and reminding us that something greater is coming.

Remember, with every blessing there is an obstacle coming. With every obstacle there is a blessing coming. If you have FAITH to reach out and grab the blessing, you must have FAITH to go through the obstacle. The more you suffer, the more you grow. What the enemy had intended to be evil, God intentionally allowed it for your good. Many who receive blessings in life without obstacles are ungrateful for what they have. When you face an obstacle, you become thankful and humble when you receive the blessing because you realize the sacrifice and pain it takes to endure things for God.

My advice to you is to continue exercising your faith daily and for the rest of your life, just as you would exercise your body at the gym when looking for different results. God will continue to show you how powerful He is and where He is taking you. Keep seeking God and He will show you your purpose. Keep asking God to lead and direct you, and trust me, He will do so. The ultimate question is: ARE YOU READY TO EXERCISE YOUR FAITH as He leads? God will continue to test your faith, and you must pass the tests. It is not easy, but it's worth it.

May the God of hope fill you with all joy and peace in believing, so that by the power of the Holy Spirit you may abound in hope. [Romans 15:13]

Chapter 5

Prayer

Paul commands: ¹⁶ Rejoice evermore. ¹⁷ Pray without ceasing. ¹⁸ In everything give thanks: for this is the will of God in Christ Jesus concerning. [1 Thessalonians 5:16-18]

Prayer is a must, a critical part of our everyday lives. If you are missing prayer in your daily life, I want to encourage and challenge you to start praying at the beginning of each day for the next thirty days.

For the first seven days, pray for about five minutes at the beginning of each day. The next seven days, pray for ten minutes. The following seven days, pray for fifteen minutes. For the next seven days, pray for twenty minutes, and on the last two days, pray for twenty-five minutes.

Each day or each week, make a list of things you want to pray for or focus on in prayer. You can add things to your list when things come up, and you can also take things off your list when God answers your prayers. Also, I encourage you to get a devotional or find a new scripture to meditate and focus on each day.

Reading a devotional or a new scripture every day will help you learn the Word, gain a closer relationship with God, increase your testimony, find wisdom, receive guidance, and hear God. As we meditate on the scriptures, they become a part of us. Once that happens, things will change in your prayer life. The Spirit's intercession is tied to God's will, which is tied to scripture. In other words, your prayers will begin to change without you even realizing it. You may think you know what you want, but God knows what you need. Your prayer and your life need to be tied to God's will, and this will lead you there.

One of the things I love about Jesus is that He intercedes on our behalf even when we don't realize it or ask for it. Romans 8:27 states: "The Spirit pleads for us believers in harmony with God's own will." As you read this book, you will see the more I prayed for healing for my child, the more my prayers shifted. This began to change the more I read the Word, meditated on scriptures, and prayed without ceasing. As I sought God, the Holy Spirit interceded on my behalf.

Praying without ceasing—praying about everything through everything—is something we all should do. Your day should already begin with prayer, but you can also pray throughout the day while brushing teeth, cooking, driving, working, and shopping. You can also pray before paying bills, before eating, and before making an important decision, etc. When praying, you do not have to be on the knees, head bowed, eyes closed position. Praying without ceasing is not praying all day every day, but it refers to an attitude of God-consciousness and God-surrender that we carry with us from the time we wake up to the time we go to bed.

In every second of our lives, we should be aware that God is omnipresent, omnipotent, all powerful, all wonderful, and forever knowing. He is with us, dynamically involved and tied in our thoughts and actions. God is everywhere at the same time, and He has unlimited power and can do anything. Prayer should be our first response to every fearful situation, obstacle, worried thought, and/or unwanted trial put before us. Prayer should come naturally like breathing. Just as it takes no thought or force to breathe, that is exactly how prayer should be. Prayer is our number one source to reach God and is our most powerful weapon.

Let's be honest. Most of us were not taught how to pray. If so, it was not something deeply engrained into us. As a child, I was taught a simple prayer to say at grace and before bed. I also learned the Lord's Prayer from one of my aunts. Despite that, I don't remember the importance of prayer being expressed to me. In the Bible, Paul commands us, "Do not be anxious about anything, but in everything by prayer and supplication with thanksgiving let your requests be made known to God." [Philippians 4:6]

My pregnancy with Royalty was full of prayer and petition, along with thanksgiving. I had some anxious moments, but I learned through prayer and reading the Bible to give my worries and thoughts to God. My entire pregnancy, I prayed and prayed. Most days, I prayed without ceasing. I purchased prayer books strictly on healing. I studied healing, sickness, disease, and the words God said in the Bible about it. I learned so much I hadn't known.

I filled my mind reading testimonies in the Bible and listening to people who had been healed from God. Throughout my pregnancy, God gave me strength, wisdom, power, and peace that I did not understand. Reading Biblical stories and watching videos of people testifying about God's healing power gave me faith that if He had done it before, He could do it again. So I did not worry much about what the doctors wanted me to worry about, which was the "death" of my unborn child. As I learned more about God and He interceded on my behalf, my prayers changed.

They sounded something like this: "Lord, let your will be done in my baby's life. Father, I trust you but help my unbelief. Lord, I give you my child to do your will." I found rest in God's word and the intimate relationship that had developed with Him. You should try it.

God will give you peace that no man can understand. Sometimes I did not understand the peace, but it was there. It came with seeking God, following His will, finding comfort in His word, and praying daily. When I shared my testimony with others, they'd say, "I don't know how you are going through that. You are strong. I would have given up." They did not understand my peace. I acknowledged God and let them know it was all because of Him. I gave—and continue to give—all the glory to God. When you seek Him, you shall find Him.

***And the peace of God, which surpasses all understanding, will guard your hearts and your minds in Christ Jesus.* [Philippians 4:7]**

Chapter 6

The Fear of Letting Things and People Go When They No Longer Serve You Any Purpose

This title is deep, and we all struggle with this. It can be scary, but on the other end, it could be the best thing to do. Your happiness, joy, peace, and success in God can be on the opposite side of that fear of letting go of certain people and situations. I wanted to touch on this in my book, not only because it was important in my journey while pregnant, but this is important, too, in your walk with Christ.

Not everyone needs to go to the next level with you, and not everyone will go to the next level with you. It is important to ask God who needs to be in your life and who does not. Ask God to graciously remove these people from your life. It is important for your growth and the new level God is trying to take you to. You cannot be bound by relationships and things of the past walking into your future. The best advice I have for you is, "You need to cut it."

When you let it go, it will seem hard because your flesh wants what is comfortable and common, so it will tell you it is okay to compromise. It is not okay to compromise your calling and your life for what is common and comfortable at the moment. This will only get you into situations you have no way of getting yourself out of. Then you will have no choice but to call on the Lord. I cannot express how important it is to let go of situations and people that weigh you down. The more you read my story, the more you will see God do new things in me when I started to be obedient to Him. I had to go through a lot in order to learn a lot and grow a lot. It was all for the better. It taught me how important it is to be obedient to God and to kill my will daily.

For many reasons, I was afraid of letting go of Royalty's father and our relationship. Both our names were on the lease where we lived, I was early in my pregnancy, and I had quit one job and took a leave of absence from another due to car troubles. Brian sometimes said he was "sorry" when he made mistakes and we argued. He wanted to marry me and said he was in love with me. Now that I look back, he sold me all types of dreams from the beginning to the end.

However, at some point I realized the longer I stayed, the more hell I would endure. I also knew I couldn't tolerate being disrespected and being called "bitch." Though it wasn't a word he used often, I can definitely recall at least one time. This is a word that is very disrespectful to me. I have never allowed any man I dated to call me this, and I was not going to start in this relationship.

I finally accepted the reality that I was pregnant by an immature boy and that our relationship would not work. I accepted that things would not change until he was ready to work on himself. But first, he had to admit to himself that he had issues, accept he had issues, and lean on God for guidance, wisdom, understanding, and deliverance.

After our and last biggest altercation, I gave him chance after chance to say and do all the right things to keep me with him. My flesh wanted me to stay, but God wanted me to leave. It took me a few days but I listened to the Holy Spirit. Without telling him, I started getting things in order to move out while he was at work. I thought leaving while he was at work would be the most peaceful route given his anger issues and me not having guts to tell him. I wanted to believe I had the guts and that I was done, but a part of me still hoped and wished things would dramatically change for the better.

He had no idea of my plans though I think he sensed I wanted to leave. Since I wasn't working, he knew I didn't have the finances to do so, but he underestimated me. I made call after call trying to put things together. One of my friends, who didn't want me in the situation anymore, bought the ticket for me. To this day, I'm still appreciative of her because she was a huge blessing in my time of need. Others helped me with funds and the adjustment of settling back in Chicago. I truly appreciate everyone who allowed God to use them in this way.

The days before I left were full of constant disagreements that lead to arguments and hurtful words. Some people say you can't have the good without the bad in the world. Along with the arguments were lots of buttering up, sweet texts, loving whispers in my ear, make-up sex, dreams cast from him, lies, fantasies, and more arguments. We just couldn't get it together.

I finally had enough after a conversation about our relationship and the diagnosis the doctor gave me, both which happened around the same time. I will never forget what Brian said: "Well, if we go back to the doctor to follow up and the doctor says the same thing, we should just get the abor—" Angry, I did not let him finish. I couldn't believe what he was about to say.

I knew in that moment he was talking out of anger and pettiness. I had learned not long before this that when he was upset, he would say anything to hurt my feelings. He didn't figure I had anywhere to go or the strength to leave him. Maybe, too, he wanted to say as many hurtful things as he could so I would leave.

Honestly, looking back, I think most of it was a lack of maturity on his end, being caught in the moment, not having great communication skills, treating me like he felt on the inside, and treating me how other women allowed him to treat them, which I wasn't doing. The abortion comment couldn't have pierced my heart any deeper, especially after everything we were going through. At that moment, I thought back to the beginning when he'd reassured me that no matter what the doctors said, that we would trust God.

After that conversation, I left the house to make a few phone calls. I called my friend to see if she had purchased the ticket and, if she had, the time of the flight. I telephoned and texted multiple people asking for a ride to the airport since my car was no longer working. The flight was leaving at 6 a.m. the following morning, and everyone seemed too busy or unable to pick me up. I was so serious about leaving that I wouldn't have minded being dropped off that very minute and spending the night at the airport.

God always has things worked out. In the midst of this chaos and my pained heart, I called another friend who immediately picked me up, and another friend sent me more money than I had asked her to send. I was more than thankful and more than ready to leave. I was hurt, but I pretended to be okay and held everything in because I didn't want to cause extra stress on my unborn child.

However, I had to accept that the relationship was over. We kept trying to give life to a dead situation, and I had to learn to let it go before I reached a point where I was completely broken from the problems projected on me and everything that comes along with staying in a dead situation.

If I stayed, I would be dead but operating in a living body. I could not imagine living like that for the rest of my life, so I had to leave as soon as possible. It hurt so bad to leave, but it also felt great and empowering. I knew I was doing what God wanted me to do and not what I wanted to do. I also knew this relationship no longer served a purpose in my life. I looked at my situation and decided I would rather leave and grow, than stay and die.

Set your heart on God and reach out to him. [Job 11:13]

Throughout this entire chaotic episode, I prayed to God, asking Him for guidance, strength, hope, peace, understanding, wisdom, love, joy, and healing over my unborn child's body. Brian and I had been given the diagnosis of our child during the beginning of this chaos, and this was also when God revealed to me that the relationship was dead.

God had to bring me all the way back to Chicago so I could see what I had to let go of and why it was essential to let go in that very moment.

God knew how much I could handle and how much He would allow, so He let Brian push the limits. That's ultimately why I left: because God allowed certain things to happen that caused so much pain I could not take it anymore. If it wasn't for God and simply up to me, I am sure I would have stayed longer. The relationship had died long ago; I just hadn't accepted it.

Remember, I was only twelve weeks pregnant and had received our baby's fatal diagnosis. Imagine being twelve weeks pregnant, in an unhealthy relationship, and making the decision to leave without knowing WHAT and HOW. I knew in my spirit if I had God I would be okay. I knew if I stayed with Brian it was only because it was easier to stay. I had to leave, not only for myself but for my unborn child. I had to be in a healthy environment. Brian wanted me to stay silent and ignore the problems in our relationship. He wanted me to agree with everything he said and every decision he made. He wanted me to submit to him and put all my trust in him. And I didn't. I spoke up for myself, my unborn child, and for what I believed in. I spoke up for the things I valued, and I demanded to be respected.

Some of you may be dealing with people who want you to remain silent in your current relationships. Maybe it's a boyfriend, spouse, family member, friend, coworker, or peer, but if you feel you need to speak up, do so. Speak up and have healthy confrontation. Silence can cost a lot, such as joy, peace, happiness, growth, blessings, and a relationship with Christ. Don't subject your happiness for someone else's. Don't stop yourself from receiving blessings from the Lord because you are still in a relationship, job, and/or place He told you no longer served you any good, if it ever did in the first place. Stop holding onto the fear of the unknown, and let go of things and people you don't need.

Fear of the unknown is what keeps us in relationships, places, jobs, and doing things we no longer need to do. Once you realize it's time to move on and grow, MOVE. Don't wait. Don't stay stagnant. Don't allow your fleshly desires to talk you out of what your spirit tells you to do. Be careful who you are connected to. God pulls you to save you. You keep fighting the pull. Run for your life. Move fast and don't look back. Staying connected to the wrong things and people after having been given wisdom and instructions from the Holy Spirit to leave is called foolish and will lead to destruction. The Bible says there is warning before destruction.

When you run, run far away. Go to places you have never been before. Don't run to anyone or anything on the same level you are on. Go to higher places or you will end up back in the old places. Stop coming up with excuses why you can't because you will talk yourself out of the challenge. Your words are powerful, so watch what you say during this challenge. By speaking certain things, you will give life to certain things that need to stay dead.

You don't see how big you are, so you keep running to small things and people. God is shifting you to get a different view. He wants to take you higher so you can look back on the places you were and the people you were with, so you can see how trifling they are and that they are not on your level. Don't stay in the same places. Go higher. Take your prayer life higher. Take your worship higher. Apply higher. Reach for new heights.

You have to find joy in your present sufferings. [Luke 21:28]

[17] I love those who love me, and those who seek me find me [18] with me are riches, and honor, enduring wealth and prosperity. [Proverbs 8:17-18]

Chapter 7

Realize When You Are Being Tested by God

In life, we are tested daily by God and Satan. You must be able to decipher between the two. Who is testing you? When you realize who's testing you, it allows you to handle it accordingly. Regardless of the test and regardless of who is testing you, you must be prepared. There are many ways of being prepared when you are being tested.

One way to get prepared is through prayer. You must seek God first each day. God will be able to give you guidance and wisdom through your tests. You will become prepared by covering yourself with the Armor of God. The Armor of God I am referring to is scripture(s) reading, meditating on the scripture(s), and prayer.

In my twenty-six years, I am just now realizing and experiencing the importance of fasting when you need God to give you exact instructions and wisdom. You can also fast when you do not have an explicit question for God but seek a more intimate relationship. Fasting is abstaining from food, drink, social media, or another choice in order to focus on a period of spiritual growth. Basically, we deny something of the flesh to glorify God, to improve our spirit, and go deeper in prayer.

Every time I need God, I pray and find scripture(s) to read. When you read scriptures and pray, God will give you guidance, wisdom, peace, understanding, and revelation, and He will fulfill all your needs at the time. Not always what you want but surely what you need.

When I first found out my baby had fluid in her brain, the spirit of worry took over me. When I arrived home from the hospital, something hit me and I cried in sadness. I had a moment, but when God put me back together, He reminded me that He did not give me the spirit of worry or fear. So I prayed and cried out to God for wisdom. I read the Word for instruction and to remind myself how great our God is. I also reached out to people for prayer over my unborn child, myself, and Brian.

Immediately after praying, reading the Word of God, and reaching out to prayer warriors, a peace came over me. God sent me comfort in my time of need just as He always does. He sent messages of encouragement, strength, peace, and joy through many different people I knew, even strangers. God held me close and took away my fear, worry, anxiety, and doubt. He replaced my pain and worries with faith. ***Now faith is confidence in what we hope for and assurance about what we do not see.* [Hebrews 11:1]**

I knew in that moment that this was ultimately a test of my faith from God. God wanted to see how much I believed in Him no matter how my situation appeared. It was hard to grasp the whole concept of what I was going through so I leaned on God. The fact that I knew it was a spiritual test and a test of my faith meant I could not give up or lose hope. If God put me through it, it was for a reason. I did not know the exact reason at the time, but later I was given revelation from God.

When faced with obstacles, it is important to know what you are dealing with. First of all, sickness is not of God. Sickness is of the devil. The enemy comes to kill, steal, and destroy. He wants our peace, mind, body, soul, and spirit. We cannot let the enemy win. We have to fight the enemy with God. God is always with us.

It is also important to know that if we are under attack by the enemy, God has to give the enemy permission to attack us. I know it sounds crazy, but it is the truth. God allows things in our lives to happen so He can get the glory. Everything we experience is for a reason, but only God knows the reasons.

I'm glad I was able to see early on that I was attacked to have my faith tested. Once I accepted that, which was early in the trial, I had to prepare myself. I had no idea what I would go through during this journey, but I was willing. I knew it would not be easy. I could not fail God as I had prior to this pregnancy.

Going through this journey, I was reminded of the Book of Job in the Bible. If you have not read the Book of Job, I encourage you to do so. I read the Book of Job in college during a rough time in my life. I felt stuck and didn't know where to go or what to do next. I was rebuilding my relationship with God and went to a friend for guidance on what books of the Bible to read.

My friend advised me to read Job. She said I reminded her of Job. Job had lost everything in the Bible, including his wife and children. However, Job did not lose his faith in God. At the time, I was not in the best place. I didn't have much in the way of possessions and was losing everything else in my life as well. However, like Job, I still had my faith. I continued to lean on God and trust Him during the difficult times. I had the mindset: *I know I am going through this for a reason. Things will get better and God is always with me.*

I will be with you even to the end of the age. [Matthew 28:20]

This mindset kept me focused on God and life's brighter side. I tried to remain positive for the most part. Instead of looking at and focusing on the negatives and my situation, I remained humble. I believe this will take you far in life. Life can never get the best of you when you focus on positives instead of negatives.

I am not saying completely ignore the obstacles as if they're not present. I truly believe you go through things to teach you lessons, so you must pay attention to the test and be aware of lessons you must learn. Then, when you are tested again, you will pass the test. God will give you the same test more than once if you don't pass it. The question is: Will you pass the test? How many times will you fail? Will you remain humble, positive, and faithful to God?

In the Book of Job, the devil asked God for permission to take everything away from Job. The devil tried to convince God that Job would curse God if the devil took everything away, so God gave the devil permission to take everything away from Job. The devil took his children, wife, and livestock. Job lived off his livestock. Everything he had and everyone he'd ever loved was gone. Job still did not curse God. Job kept his faith.

We must learn to walk by faith and not by sight. When we go through trials, we are tempted to believe what is physically in front of us is going to be the outcome of our situation. This is a trick of the devil. If he can get us to believe that God is not with us, he has won. We need to also understand that if we walk by faith and stand on the Word of God, our true reward is not on earth but in Heaven. Sometimes as humans we want to focus so much on the severity of the test that we lose sight of God.

Some people want to believe that God doesn't allow bad things to happen in our lives. Individuals get mad at God and curse his name. Others have so much hatred in their hearts toward God due to situations and people taken from them. It is sad to witness. Their limited perspective of their lives here on earth hinders them from the light of eternity.

God allows everything to happen for a reason. We will never get the full details while we are here on earth. God is with you through every trial, tribulation, and obstacle. God will reward you double for everything you lose. In the Book of Job, Job received the blessings God had stored for him only after he went through his obstacles, received scars, endured pain, and forgave his friends and prayed for them.

And the LORD restored the fortunes of Job when he prayed for his friends, and the LORD increased all that Job had twofold. [Job 42:10]

God can and will do the same for you. As you are going through your tests, ask God what he needs you to learn. God may need you to learn something about yourself, friends, family, and/or simply God Himself. God always wants to make His presence known in our lives. Reach out to God. Do not run away and try to hide. God wants to give you a new testimony to share with others while giving Him all the glory. You can pass this test! Stay humble, pray, seek God first, and remain positive. Don't give up on God, because He won't give up on you.

This is only a test designed to get your prayer life where it used to be. God solves all our problems. Our kingdoms will fall when we try to solve it. If we do it on our own, we will mess up. It is essential to trust God. Give God enough respect to call on Him for help. Stop calling on your friends and family; they can't help you like God can.

Chapter 8

Be Careful What You Promise God

In her deep anguish Hannah prayed to the Lord, weeping bitterly. And she made a vow saying, "Lord Almighty, if you will only look on your servant's misery and remember me, and not forget your servant but give her a son, then I will give him to the Lord for all the days of his life, and no razor will ever be used on his head." [1 Samuel 1:10-11]

So in course of time Hannah became pregnant and gave birth to a son. She named him Samuel, saying, "Because I asked the Lord for him." [1 Samuel 1:20]

Before being pregnant with my daughter Royalty, I was in a relationship with a man named Tyrese. When he asked me to move in with him, I accepted. I spent almost every night there anyhow. I really was interested in him and our relationship grew quickly.

I loved the way he treated me and how well we clicked. I perceived that God was the head of both our lives. Together, we went to Bible study every Wednesday and church almost every Sunday. Tyrese supported me in a lot of things. *He could be the one*, I thought.

Several months prior to my moving in with Tyrese, I had been involved in a motor vehicle accident where my car was totaled. A few months before that accident, I was involved in another accident and another car I owned was totaled. I was an in-home Case Manager for a mental health agency in Atlanta, Georgia, and wasn't working as much as I wanted or needed to after both accidents. My job duties entailed a wide range of things. I wore multiple hats, to say the least, and my car was how I got from point A to B.

After a year at this job, I became overwhelmed with the company's unprofessionalism and didn't feel I could grow there anymore. I desired a job with more organization and professionalism. Instead of in-home services that required excessive driving, I wanted a position closer to home, where I didn't have as much driving and where God could use me. I prayed and prayed for a new job.

It's funny how God works. I was placed at another company through my employment because I had a client who was with that company, never knowing I would eventually transition there. A couple of months later, God blessed me with a job at that company, which offered almost everything I was looking for.

Also, at that time I found out I was pregnant. Yes, pregnant. You are thinking that is a blessing, and it truly was. I was very thankful to God for blessing me with my child. However, I was still shocked. No one at my job ever knew about my pregnancy. I told my mom and very few family and friends.

The title of this chapter is "Be Careful What You Promise God." I also want you to understand that prayer is powerful and to be careful what you pray for. There is a permissive will of God and a perfect will of God. The permissive will is our will and what we want. The perfect will is God's will for our lives. God will grant us through our prayers things of our permissive will for His purposes of bringing us back to Him and understanding that His will is greater for our lives than our own.

Before finding out that I was pregnant, one day during my quiet time with God I prayed and cried out to Him. My heart was heavy and I wanted change. I asked God for a lot of things. One thing in particular I asked for was a son. I did just as Hannah had done in the Bible in the above scriptures and decided to give the prayer a try. I had recently read this story in the Bible and heard many other women's testimonies of how they prayed to God and asked God for sons and/or daughters and how God blessed them with exactly what they prayed for.

I knew the power of God but truly didn't believe God would answer my prayer for a son as quickly as He did. At that time in my life, I was heavy with emotions from near and far and didn't know how to deal with everything. I thought I had been dealing with issues and thought most were gone. Somehow, the feelings of hurt, guilt, shame, defeat, neglect, abandonment, rejection, loneliness, anger, confusion, and doubt, along with the lack of family's love and support crept back on me. Looking back, most of the times when faced with adversity, I swept it under a rug and never truly dealt with my emotions as I needed to.

I suddenly longed to be a mother. I desired to love my children as I wanted to be loved, and I would fulfill that because I yearned to be loved by my mother and father. I wanted children because I knew I would be a great mother. I had so much love inside me and desired to give this love to my children.

Also playing into my eagerness to have a child was the fact that everyone around me and those I grew up with had children, and I was one of the last few without. Though I was eager, in no way would I make it happen with just anyone. I wasn't that thirsty!

However, I had been in a relationship with Tyrese for some time, we were living together, and we were in love. I thought he was the one, remember? And I thought we would eventually marry. Neither of us had children from prior relationships. I say all this to show my feelings, but a lot was happening on the inside that I had no idea about. My flesh and my spirit were at war with one another because I wanted to get married before having children; my flesh didn't care about my situation and how it looked. My flesh was willing to push my values and what I knew God wanted for me to the side to subside the pain and emotions I was having.

When I prayed at the time like Hannah had, I specifically prayed for a son. I felt I had never had a man in my life who truly loved me, and I suppose I wanted to fill that void. I have three living brothers and one deceased, but I never felt love from them. They'd never been close to me and were not present in my life at that time—meaning, we never talked to one another. For years, I reached out to them to no avail and accepted that they were just "too busy" in their own lives to make time for me. I had thought I was "okay" with it, but that was my flesh lying to me again. Truly, I was deeply hurt by their actions and didn't understand why our relationships were so dead.

Another reason for wanting a son was because my biological father had never been in my life, and when I opened that door, he never showed he loved me. This was a lot deeper than I knew at the time. I thought accepting people for who they were and telling myself, "It's okay," "Fuck them," "I don't need anybody," that I was okay with the situation. But that was another lie. The enemy wanted me to believe that I was okay and I wasn't because my unhappiness showed up in my habits, relationships, thoughts, and actions. Once again, however, at the time I was unaware of these things.

I was the only one of my siblings without children. I had seven nieces and no nephews, so I thought if I had a boy, my family would love me more and give me the attention I had always desired. My baby could potentially solve a lot of problems.

But mainly, I just wanted to love my child, receive love from my child, and raise him to be a man of God. In today's society, we lack a lot of positive, spiritual, and strong men of God, so I knew my baby boy would be all those things. My baby would make a change in this world and in my life.

27 I prayed for this child, and the Lord granted me what I asked of him. 28 So now I give him to the Lord. For his whole life he will be given over to the Lord..." [1 Samuel 1:27]

When I think back, you could say I was underestimating the power of God. I believed that God could do it, but I wasn't thinking of the immediate future. I knew God. I loved God. God blessed me daily. God performed miracles in my life. God healed me. God provided for me. I thanked God daily. I praised God daily. I read my word here and there. God was everything I needed Him to be, but I didn't know if He would bless me the way I asked, and if He did, when He would bless me.

God did just what I asked Him—and suddenly, at that.

In my prayer, I told God almost exactly what Hannah had. I said, "If you give me a son, I will raise him as a king under your throne." I promised God that if he gave me a son, my son would live for Him. I believed my own words as they left my mouth. At the time, I didn't know the depth and power of my words.

Hannah followed through with her prayer and promise to God, but I didn't follow through with my prayer and promise to God. I was pregnant with a purpose, and I failed to see that. When the pressures of life kept hitting me, I failed the very test I had prayed for. God had prepared me for such a time, but I failed. I felt incompetent and helpless. God whispered in my ear and told me he was with me and always would be, but I believed the demons that attacked me.

I looked at my current situation and the waves that crashed on me from everywhere. I was beaten in every way, shape, and form, which killed my purpose. The enemy wanted me to believe I wasn't equipped to be a mother at that time. My situation changed and worsened suddenly. Have you ever heard, "It must get worse before it gets better?" Well, I guess that's what was taking place, but I wasn't looking at it like that at the time.

I leaned on God during this difficult time, asking Him for instructions. God gave me directions to do what He wanted me to, which is just as Hannah did in the scriptures. Instead, I did what I wanted to do based on HOW my situation looked. I wasn't thinking back on all the times God had been there for me and all the messes He brought me out of. I wasn't thinking about all the times He saved me from the hand of the enemy. I only thought about how hard my situation appeared before my eyes.

Tyrese, the very man I thought who loved me and who I put my trust in, began to reject me and our unborn child. This started months after we found out I was pregnant. We had discussed and accepted the situation, and I thought he was happy about the child. The man I thought could be the one changed overnight. He changed his positive attitude about me to a negative attitude. Some days he wouldn't speak to me. Before the pregnancy, we spent most of our time outside of work together. We worked out, went to church, worked on our business, and dated. Suddenly, we were spending less time together and less time talking. Most days and nights, he wouldn't utter a word.

When Tyrese eventually talked to me, I couldn't believe the words that came from his mouth. His words were sharp like a knife. He eventually told me he didn't want the child anymore. I was shocked, angry, sad, and mad—all the emotions you can think of. I was especially confused because the first few months he hadn't acted that way.

But suddenly he changed his mind and expressed hatred toward me. I was in so much shock I couldn't take it all in. Immediately I said, "I am going to keep my baby no matter what." I continued for a long time with this thought, not believing he would pressure me into getting an abortion. He played mind games, as well, and at the time, you couldn't have told me he would win this mental attack or convince me to abort my baby. If you had, I probably would have slapped you.

During this time, I confided in friends, who encouraged me to do the right thing and to keep my baby.

One day, Tyrese told me I had to leave his house immediately and he didn't care where I went. He even told me he didn't want to be a part of our child's life and that I could file for child support because "I know that's what you plan to do anyway." He even accused me of searching though his stuff for his social security number while he was at work. I was appalled at his remarks, schemes, tactics, and actions. I was confused, lost, hurt, and ashamed.

I prayed. I cried out to God. I asked God for understanding, help, support, wisdom, and love. I felt I had been tossed to the ground, where people threw huge blocks on top of me, one after another.

It was a never-ending story. Every day was different living with this man. Some days he would talk; other days he wouldn't. Sometimes he cooked for me and would do small things to show he cared. Overall, I was so out of it I didn't know what to do.

This was my first time in a situation like this. All I could think about was my image, and I let the enemy's instructions linger in my thoughts. I started to believe what the enemy told me. I fell into the trap of the enemy even though I should have been prepared in every way. I felt God had already equipped, prepared, and purposed me for such a circumstance.

How was I going to get through this? I felt so alone and that I'd failed everyone including myself. I thought about my situation. I had entered into a relationship, moved into the home of a man I barely knew, and allowed myself to believe I knew him, thinking this man really loved me and that "he could be the one." I was falling in love with potential. I was falling in love with what our relationship could potentially be, the man he could potentially be, the husband and father he could potentially be.

I know I am not alone in this. Most women fall in love with potential. We have hopes and see that things could potentially be greater than they are. If I haven't learned that going through this test, I have learned it now. You cannot fall in love with potential because that can potentially stop you from going to places where God leads you. Would you rather fail people or God?

The moment you've all been waiting for: Yes, after much thought and my flesh convincing me it was the right thing to do, I had the abortion. But before you judge me, look at your own flaws.

Now back to the point I was getting to. In my mind, I made the decision for many reasons I felt strongly about. All in all, I couldn't see myself in that position because of all the obstacles that lay before me.

A few months into the pregnancy, Tyrese put so much pressure on me and expressed that "we" were not ready for this. The beginning was all good when we found out. Hell, the sex was good when we were doing it, but then all of a sudden he didn't want the baby.

Talk about a rug pulled from under my feet! And then, when I sat down, somebody piled a bunch of bricks on top of me. I couldn't believe the things he said, the way he acted, and how he truly felt. I prayed, cried, prayed, and cried more and more. I was told to keep my baby so many times by God, but I did what I wanted to do—well, really, what Tyrese wanted me to do.

You can't believe it, right? You could not look at me and see that I had an abortion. Well, that is right. I would not expect you to be able to see that. You don't know half of what I suffered, so never judge a book by its cover.

After I made the decision to abort, I felt I had failed God because I did not follow through on my promise to Him, and I didn't know what that would mean between me and God. I didn't know how I would rise from that and didn't understand the consequences that could come from broken promises to God. I just knew that it would not be good.

I felt so alone and down and horrible. Throughout this test, God revealed to me, "This is the biggest test of your faith. Do you truly believe in me like you say you do?" However, I still had the abortion and basically failed the test.

God urged me to write about this journey for so many reasons. He wanted me to show others who have been in my position that they are not alone. He also revealed to me that women I knew had abortions and were ashamed to admit it. He informed me that many women deal with guilt, hurt, loss, and pain from abortions. In society today, this issue is prevalent but not talked about like it should. So many women are ashamed to share their stories because of judgment that may come from it.

I want you to know you are not alone. It was a mistake. God wants you to repent and ask Him for forgiveness. God will and has already forgiven you. God wants you to forgive yourself and move forward. Don't beat yourself up. God still loves you. God will continue to love you. God wants you to cry out to Him and give it all to Him so you can move forward. God will have mercy on you. Remember, you went through this for a reason. You might not know why now, but you will find out.

Also, don't allow anyone to stop you from helping someone by not sharing your testimony because of fear of judgment and shame. No sin is greater than the next, and God is the one who will judge you one day. Other's opinions don't even matter. The more you focus on what other people may say about you, the more you will block yourself from moving forward and allowing God to use you. God can use you even when you feel as if he can't.

God wants you to be transparent to others about your battles, obstacles, trails, and tests. Even more so, God wants you to be transparent to others about your victories and His grace and mercy over your life. God will show your gifts once you open your mouth for him. If God has not yet given you understanding as to why you have been through the trials and tribulations, He will reveal that to you in many ways. God wants to hear from you. I reach God during my quiet time with Him—through prayer, reading the Bible, writing to Him, talking to Him, going to church, listening to online sermons, and through prophets. When I do that, He reveals things to me.

God talks to each of us in special ways. God has revealed to me why I had the abortion I never thought I'd have. For a long time, I carried guilt until He gave me comfort and said some things were not really in my control. I say "not really" because I was unaware what was going on at the time, so I had no control as I thought I did in my fleshy mind. I was under attack by Satan and I failed to use the armor of God as I needed to get through the situation and have victory. However, everything happens for a reason.

God still loves you when you are not obedient to Him, when you backslide, when you deny Him, and when you make mistakes. God wants us all to be sorry in our hearts and repent for our sins. God forgives us and forgets about our sins. God casts all our sins into the sea of forgetfulness so He no longer remembers them and does not hold grudges over us. God is not that type of God. However, God does discipline His children just as you would discipline your child, but that is another chapter.

Matthew 5:33-37

Oaths

[33] *Again, you have heard that it was said to the people long ago, "Do not break your oath, but fulfill to the Lord the vows you have made."* [34] *But I tell you, do not swear an oath at all: either by heaven, for it is God's throne;* [35] *or by the earth, for it is his footstool; or by Jerusalem, for it is the city of the Great King.*

³⁶ And do not swear by your head, for you cannot make even one hair white or black. ³⁷ All you need to say is simply "Yes" or "No"; anything beyond this comes from the evil one.

If you have not learned anything from this chapter, "Be Careful What You Promise God," one thing you should take from it is not to make promises to God that you cannot keep. If God instructs you to do something, be obedient and stand on His promises no matter how your situation may look.

¹ Hear me, Lord, and answer me, for I am poor and needy. ² Guard my life, for I am faithful to you; save your servant who trusts in you. You are my God; ³ have mercy on me, Lord, for I call to you all day long. ⁴ Bring joy to your servant, Lord, for I put my trust in you. ⁵ You, Lord, are forgiving and good, abounding in love to all who call to you. ⁶ Hear my prayer, Lord; listen to my cry for mercy. ⁷ When I am in distress, I call to you, because you answer me. [Psalm 86:1-7]

Chapter 9

Pressures

There is only so much pressure that you can handle in life.

While going through my pregnancy journey with Royalty, there were times I couldn't handle anything more. I had more pressure on me than I could keep up with, which included going alone to the doctor, accepting the end of the relationship with her dad, Brian, and the reality of my situation. On top of that, I was unemployed and relocating back to my mother's house after being gone for about nine years.

I can honestly say that once I made the decision to leave Brian and put my focus primarily on God, everything changed. I applied for two jobs after moving back to Chicago and got both of them in the same week. I asked God to reveal to me which one I should take, and He made it very clear.

When I started the new job, my coworkers were mean and inconsiderate. The workload on the job was heavy and demanding, and I had little to no support in such an unsafe environment. My family wasn't as supportive as I would have liked; they struggled with their own issues. My friendships were ending. I struggled financially and searched for a place to live. The doctors kept trying to convince me to end my pregnancy. Everywhere I looked and everywhere I turned, everyone seemed to be against me. Let's just say the odds were never in my favor.

After I relocated back home, I went alone to most of my doctor's appointments. Outside of the appointments, the enemy reminded me what the doctors were telling me, and I'd worry if my baby was okay.

I had been diagnosed with Lupus in September 2011 and Fibromyalgia in January 2012. Studies showed individuals afflicted with those diseases might not be able to carry a baby to term. I worried about the possibility I couldn't have kids and that my health was potentially at risk. The enemy is tricky and tried to convince me that the smallest pain in my body or my baby not moving enough signaled something wrong. I worried too much and went to the ER too often.

God is such a great God. God continued to remind me who He is and who He will always be. God is a way maker, a provider, a healer, a doctor, a father. He's my food when I'm hungry and my water when I'm thirsty.

After my diagnoses, I suffered physically, mentally, emotionally, and spiritually, but through it all, God was right by my side and with me every step of the way. God literally carried me through, so when I was faced with another health obstacle (Royalty's diagnosis), I would fight through it with my mind on Him.

God is always intentional. Being diagnosed with Lupus and Fibromyalgia right after I turned twenty-one and going through another health crisis was a difficult time for me. However, we never know the plans of the Lord. God wanted to get me closer to Him, seek Him with all my heart, show me who He truly was and the plans He had for me. Going through all the hell and pressures equipped me for greater obstacles. I fought a long, hard, good fight because of the Lord. My faith increased my relationship with God, and my testimony.

Immediately after I received the diagnoses of Lupus, God whispered to me, "I am going to heal you just like I have done for many others. And you will be able to heal others as well." I said, "Thank you, Lord. I trust you." From that moment forward, I knew I would endure much, but I knew why. I had many tests and monthly doctor visits. I was seeing rheumatologists, who are doctors trained in autoimmune diseases, which is what Lupus and Fibromyalgia are. My lab results were horrible, and I had prescriptions for hundreds of different medications, taking about thirty pills a day. In effect, I was a test dummy for doctors who knew nothing about Lupus, let alone an African American woman with Lupus. Besides that, I was depressed, lost, confused, and in pain.

At the end of 2013, I was taken off all my medications. The doctors thought they were in control but all along it was God being intentional.

I've been off medications for three years now, and my life has improved. My lab results are better than ever, and tests reveal a person with great health. I no longer have appointments with rheumatologists. I'm more active, more spiritual, more loving, more discerning, more thankful for life, and more purposeful at what I do.

God truly turned my life around when I turned from my ways, trusted Him, and gave Him the wheel in my life. Funny thing: I am not perfect and I've walked away from God plenty of times after this. However, what I love about God is that He will never give up on you. He continued to pull, tug, and push me. I love Him for that. He is the best support I have ever had and needed. He will never leave my side no matter what.

All in all, Jesus made a way. He healed me, even after the doctors told me so many horrible things about my heath and what it meant for my life! He truly is a miracle worker. Imagine experiencing God's mighty healing powers and then receiving Royalty's diagnosis and doctors trying to convince me to kill my baby. I knew what God was able to do because I experienced it firsthand. I read so many stories in the Bible about God's healing and miraculous powers. I've met people in the physical, and I had seen God do it time and time again. All these things encouraged me and gave me strength during these hard times. The questions were: God, will you do it for me again? Is this a part of your plan for my life? I know you are able, but will you heal my baby?

My sister was with me during my first doctor's appointment after I moved home. The appointment was a quick visit to a new doctor. A few days after that visit, the doctor's office called to give me an emergency appointment. I was a bit concerned and thought the doctor might tell me that he didn't want me as a patient because my pregnancy was too much for him to handle. I said a quick prayer and headed alone to the appointment. The doctor said he'd finally reviewed all the reports from my pervious doctors and emergency room visits. This new doctor sent me for a Level 2 ultrasound, so they could take a closer look to see how the baby had developed since the previous tests.

I prayed and asked God to heal my baby girl. The Holy Spirit spoke to me, telling me to get ready. I thought God was speaking with regard to Him healing my baby, so I was thirsty and went to the store and shopped to prepare for her arrival. Anytime you believe God for something, you receive it, claim it, and accept it before it manifests in the physical. The Word says to walk by faith and not by sight, so I did just that. It felt good to actually look at things on the brighter side. I had always kept a positive attitude, prayed, declared healing, and read the Word, but I still had times where fear and worry crept up on me.

I was excited for new beginnings and the birth of my baby girl and couldn't wait for the ultrasound. My mom said she wanted to go to the appointment with me. I felt pressure to say yes because I was using her car and she is "my mother," right? I would have preferred Brian or my sister to accompany me, based on our relationships at the time, but I accepted the fact that my mom was there and tried to be thankful. I did appreciate her presence and support but didn't fully embrace it as I should have.

During the level 2 ultrasound, the technician who viewed my baby was positive with a great attitude. She printed pictures of my baby and answered all my questions. Eventually, she called in the specialist, who spoke with confusion and questioned me like the last doctor, "What do you know about what is going on? Have you thought about terminating this pregnancy?" The pressure I experienced from those words was strong. Confidently, I replied, "No. I am keeping my baby. I heard that from the last doctor, and I'm aware from the last ultrasound how my baby is developing."

I needed to stay strong and not break down. I actually didn't feel like crying because I was used to holding it in, and at this point, it was almost natural. Had I been alone at the appointment, I possibly would have cried, but since my mother was present, I felt pressure to hold it together. When I left the appointment after hearing again "Your child will not live, and she will die in your belly. The chances of her living are slim to none based on her development," I was broken on the inside but once again felt pressure to keep things together.

Immediately, God reminded me how He has healed so many people time and time again. I was a bit relieved but not completely. I felt the pressure to keep holding on to my faith and proclaiming that I had faith that God would save my baby. However, deep down, I sometimes questioned keeping my baby. I didn't know if God would heal my baby or not. I wanted to tell everyone God would heal her, and I did.

I do believe that God can heal you from anything because He has healed me, but I didn't completely know if He would heal my baby. Throughout this journey, I had to continually remind myself that this was a test. I had to consistently reach out to people for prayers, pray faithfully, read the Word, stay in God's presence, follow God, seek Him, have faith, trust Him, have more faith, continue to trust Him, and be strong in my weakness.

I did the only thing I knew, which was to fight this pressure and to resist it from taking control over me. I had to do exactly what I instructed all of you to do in earlier chapters and what I have continually instructed you to do, which was to pray and read the Word. It got to the point I needed to share my story because I had so much faith God could and would heal my baby. I knew I could pray all day, but the Word says faith without works is dead. In a sense, I felt it was something I must do in order to help God heal my baby.

According to the scripture and the way most readers interpret it, even though we believe God to answer our prayer(s), we still have responsibility in the situation. It is important that while you wait for your blessing you do what He needs from you.

During that time, I had been introduced to vitamins that could possibly help my baby, as well as my health. I researched the vitamins and prayed over them and was led by the Holy Spirit to purchase them. However, I wasn't working and didn't have any money. And, of course, the vitamins cost an arm and a leg. Listening to the Holy Spirit, I set up a GoFundMe account, where I asked people for help to purchase the vitamins.

This was unusual for me. I had to set aside my pride and ask for financial assistance from others, especially strangers. At first, I didn't want to give many details of my situation or what the doctors had said, but I was obedient to what God told me to do.

My goal was $1,000 because that was the cost of the vitamins the Homeopathic doctor suggested. Within the first few hours, I had received about $400, but not nearly enough. God reminded me that patience will bless me. After a few weeks, I had over $700 in donations. I decided to order what I could with the money I had and order the rest when more money came in. While I was placing the order, God worked more wonders. I received a discount and price specials and had just enough money to purchase the first month's supply. I was thankful and amazed at the support I received.

God confirmed that I did the right thing and to continue to be obedient to him. I was overwhelmed and so thankful. I kept praising God and telling Him, "Thank you." This was just the beginning of the miraculous signs and blessings I would receive from God during this journey.

After I relocated back home, I felt pressure to help everybody while I wasn't working. I knew God had put me there for a purpose, so I mistakenly outstretched myself helping others. I was tired, irritable, stressed, sick, worried, and in pain but trying to hold it all together. I have always had the heart to assist others, whether family, friends, or strangers. I know what it feels like not to have any help, and I know how it feels to have too much pride to ask for assistance, so I'm always willing to help others. I also live with the mindset, "Help others when you can because you never know when you may be in need of help yourself."

Eventually, I looked for a new job. The little support I thought I had and the people I had overextended myself for were hard to find. It's like they were there to help one day and the next, magically gone. The people I had helped were ones I depended upon to help me get through my trying time, not because I thought they should be there because I had helped them, but because of words they said and promises they made. When reality revealed that these people weren't going to be there, I pretended I was okay with that.

You know that quote "You have to accept people for who they are"? I am sure you have heard it on many occasions, and I'm sure you've tried to tell yourself that when people disappoint you. So, I'm sure you'll understand that I tried to swallow the fact I could not change others. I wanted to accept and adopt that quote in my mind and heart, but it was difficult.

I felt the pressure not to be angry, but deep down inside I was hurt, sad, angry, upset, emotional, and shocked. I made those people think at the time that not helping me was not upsetting me because I depended on God for everything, which was true. But in those moments, I felt defeated. I really needed them and didn't see how I'd get things done and get to places without their help. But that's when God reminded me that He was the same God the previous day as He was that day and as He would be the following day.

I kept Brian updated on what the doctors had said at the visits even though he wasn't calling me to ask. I felt the pressure to tell him because I had convinced myself I was righteous and doing what was right in God's eyes no matter how immature I felt Brian was.

I also felt pressure to project my anger and emotions on him when I was stressed with life, not just the pregnancy. He was not as supportive as I thought he should be, so I always told him what he wasn't doing and how he was making me feel.

I felt pressure to reach out to him when images and thoughts popped in my head about our baby girl not making it. Since she was our child, he should feel the same way I felt.

Nobody knew all the details of what Brian and I were going through. Some of the people closest to me just knew things were not good between us. No one truly knew our story and our struggle. No one knew I was breaking on the inside, trying to accept my reality for what it was. No one knew I was dying on the inside. No one knew I was willing to give up my life to save my child's. No one knew I didn't know what to expect day-to-day during my pregnancy. No one knew that at every doctor's appointment the doctors focused on abortion.

No one knew the spiritual battle I was going through. No one knew how I held my head high. No one knew where my strength came from. No one knew why I suffered what I did. No one knew that even I didn't know what I was going through. No one knew the enemy tried to attack me with thoughts of an abortion and tried to convince me that God was punishing me. No one knew the enemy even used Brian to say those very words as well. Those words and thoughts pierced my mind.

In life and in our trials, we will have pressures that come from left and right. They will continue to show up and try to make you fall and give up and turn your back on God. The load seems too heavy at times, almost as if you can't take anymore and you're at your breaking point BUT FOR GOD. God always has a greater plan.

That is why it is essential when you are in the wilderness and getting scars left and right, that you are in the presence of the Lord at ALL TIMES. Continue to keep your face in the Bible, pray daily, find a network of prayer warriors, go to church consistently, and wash up in the Word daily. In doing all these things, you will graciously fight and ultimately win any battle. The Word (scriptures) and calling on God is your greatest weapon in any battle.

The enemy must be defeated when you call on that great name, Jesus. The enemy is so strategic at what he does. One of his greatest tricks is to attack your mind. If the enemy can continuously remind you of how many times you have failed, how many times God did not answer the prayer the way you wanted it, how many mistakes you have made, and how many times you have turned your back on God, he can make you depressed, sad, angry, frustrated, hopeless, worried, afraid, and so many other things.

When the enemy is trying to attack your mind, he wants to manipulate your thoughts and have control over your life. He knows you better than you know yourself. Would you believe me if I told you that demons have meetings about how to attack you? Would you believe me if I told you Satan had a book about you that contains everything that makes you happy, sad, and depressed; details regarding your purpose and your destiny; information on your family and friends; and so on? His plans are to kill, steal, and destroy in whatever way possible.

This is why it is so important to follow all the instructions I give you throughout this book. If it was not for God instructing me, leading me, and guiding me to do all these things and for me being obedient, I would have given up, lost my mind, committed suicide, aborted Royalty, become bitter, or projected my frustration, anger, confusion, and sadness onto others. But God!

I cannot take any credit for my strength while walking through this season and any other season. I have been through hell, feeling like the slaves back in the day must have felt when they were beaten daily with whips by Satan and his demons. I had endured so many scars in this season alone that I knew I looked ugly. I can truly testify to say, "Praise God, I do not look like what I have been through."

God is so good. Allow God to lead you and guide you everywhere you go. If you become obedient to Him and submit to His will, I cannot begin to tell you the places He will take you, the things you will see, and the people you will encounter. Get ready for the new levels God is about to take you to. You think that everything you have gone through was for no reason. No, it was all purposeful and designed to help create who you are in Christ. You cannot help anyone if you have never been through anything. And I am not referring to small things, but episodes where the ground under you is shaken, shifted, removed, and makes you question your faith in God. I promise you that every scar you endured was to help someone else see the glory of God. You cannot have a test without a testimony, and you cannot become successful without going through the wilderness.

Even Jesus was in the desert for forty days and forty nights. Imagine all the pressures He went through. When Jesus came to earth to show us the way, He endured so much pain, negativity, and hurt because people did not understand who He was and His purpose. People lacked their faith in God, so they definitely did not want to believe anything He said or did. Overall, Jesus had to come here to pave the way to show us who God is and how He is full of miracles, signs, and wonders. How He created the beginning and the end. How only God knows what, why, how, when, and who about everything.

And we know that in all things God works for the good of those who love him, who have been called according to his purpose. [Romans 8:28]

Chapter 10

What Would You Do If I Died?

From the time Brian and I received the diagnosis for our baby girl to the moment I gave birth, I've been faced with what seems like the most taunting question: WHAT WOULD YOU DO IF I DIED?

Limb Body Wall Complex (LBWC) is the diagnosis they gave me at twelve and a half weeks pregnant. LBWC is rare. I was told by doctors that one of every 15,000 pregnant women is diagnosed with this. In most cases, the babies don't live, so doctors automatically tell all women with this condition that their child is incompatible with life.

Doctors highly suggest termination of pregnancy to all women who are diagnosed with LBWC. Immediately when I was given the diagnosis, the doctors suggested I get an abortion. Crazy, right? However, my faith was in God. Even though the doctor used phrases during the ultrasound such as, "It looks like," "I think," "The baby is still too small to tell exactly what's going on," "I don't know what this is," "Most woman given this diagnosis terminate their baby," and "You are young, you can try again," I didn't let these scary comments stop me from allowing God to finish what He started.

The doctors told me at every appointment "Your baby will die in your stomach," and "Your baby will not be born alive." The first doctor giving us the diagnosis tried to persuade us to make the decision to kill our unborn child right then and there because of his medical experience and advice.

During the ultrasound at the time we received the diagnosis, the third appointment I'd had in a week, I watched my baby on the screen while eying the specialist as he moved the tool. He performed both a vaginal and a belly ultrasound to get a closer look at our sweet baby.

After the ultrasound, the doctor asked me to dress and for us to meet with him in the conference room next door. Really, I believed he wanted us to go into the room to talk us into killing our child. Hearing "You should kill your child" and "This baby will not live" was a very horrific moment in our lives.

Brian was sitting far away in this very dark and quiet room during the ultrasound. As I glanced at him from time to time, he was still, stiff, and quiet. The more the doctor insinuated that we should kill our sweet baby and explained the abnormalities he saw, the more uncomfortable Brian became. At one point, he wiped away tears.

At that moment, I knew he was scared, worried, hopeless, distraught, lost, and confused. I wanted to hug him and tell him that everything would be okay. But then I thought, *Why is he so far away? Why is he not right by my side especially when we received this devastating and heavy information from the specialist?*

I didn't immediately say anything to him. During every ultrasound and doctor visit, whenever I heard something was wrong with my baby,

I knew God was with me. Before going to the appointments, I prayed silently from the moment I woke up. I prayed during the car rides, sitting in the waiting rooms, and during my appointments. I asked God for strength, peace, love, comfort, support, reassurance, hope, and help. I truly felt the presence of God with me because not at one moment did fear come to mind. Sadness was my emotion, and the unknown was definitely my state of mind. However, tears would not come even if I wanted them to.

The ER Visit

Three days prior to meeting with the specialist, we went to the ER because I was having pains and wanted to check on my baby. At that time, Brian and I had been waiting for our first doctor's appointment, which was a week away and felt like forever. I wanted to see a doctor because of the Lupus and Fibromyalgia I had previously been diagnosed with and wanted to ensure I wasn't having complications from either of those.

During the visit, they performed an ultrasound to see how the baby was. After the ultrasound results, the doctors in the ER told me everything was fine and that they only found a "little" fluid in our baby's head. They referred to this as Hydrocephalus. I didn't know what it meant, but it didn't sound like good news hearing that on my first ultrasound.

That ultrasound at the ER was the very first time seeing my baby on the screen. They wouldn't allow her father to go with me, so I was alone. I wasn't in the best mood, but everything changed when I viewed my baby.

In that first moment seeing her on the screen, I instantly made a deeper connection with her. My heart grew bigger and my desire to be a mother grew stronger. I was excited and thankful, but a bit sad because her dad wasn't with me to share the moment, but I accepted it and gave thanks to God for such a marvelous creation growing in my belly.

During this visit, it hit me like a strong wind: I am someone's Mommy! I sat there thinking, *I can't wait to see my baby, touch my baby, kiss my baby, and love on my baby.*

While in the ER, I had no idea of the LBWC diagnosis. I thought about all the exciting things that come along with giving birth. The time we would spend together and the places we would go together. Though still in physical and emotional pain, and mentally exhausted, I was overwhelmed with joy. I had so many thoughts, feelings, and emotions all at once.

They eventually took me back to the room where Brian waited. Then we had to wait for the results of the tests, labs, and the ultrasound.

Brian wasn't in a great mood because we had been arguing all that morning. It was a major argument and the ultimate breaking point of our relationship. I did not know that for a fact then, however, but reflecting back, the relationship was dead at that time. We tried to revitalize it, but it would not work, and this argument solidified it for me.

While in the emergency room, we talked about the argument we had earlier that day. Low and behold, we began playing the blame game. In my perspective, the argument could have been avoided had he responded better to what had taken place right before the argument. His response had been blatantly disrespectful toward me emotionally, mentally, and physically.

In the moment, it was as if he'd forgotten I carried his child. He also forgot the pain I'd mentioned experiencing over the past few weeks. He immediately got on the phone with his "fake sister," disrespecting me, telling her our issues instead of handling it, and calling me a "BITCH," all in the same sentence. I couldn't believe he was disrespecting me like that.

I had just returned back "home" after spending a month and a half with my family. I hoped the time apart allowed him to grow and gain control over his anger, but I was wrong; he hadn't changed. He tried to convince me through phone calls and text messages that he had changed, however, and he'd show me if I returned. This wakeup call, which was literally a wakeup call from God, happened within the first twenty-four hours after my return to the home we shared together.

I was furious and immediately felt I needed to defend myself as well as "FIX IT." At that point, things were unfixable, but I did not want to fully accept that. So, as we sat in the emergency room awaiting test results, the tension was still apparent. My heart was heavy and saddened because I truly knew things were over. I wanted out, but all I could think about was how to fix it.

I thought, *If he only could see where he makes mistakes, then things can get better. Well, once he accepts it and begins to do the work on himself.* I knew I had issues too, and I wasn't the best at communicating, especially when I'm dealing with my own crises. The only way I knew to handle an issue in my own situation was to defend and protect myself. I later realized this was not healthy.

The crazy thing about this argument and all our other arguments was him trying to convince me that nothing he did was wrong. He justified everything, and I justified some of my actions as well. I had valid reasons, but that doesn't make me right. He could never hold himself accountable for his actions. I realized this shortly after we moved in together, and actually, to be honest, I knew this before we were even in a "committed relationship."

He told me one of his biggest problems was that he is never wrong. That should have been a BIG RED FLAG, but for some reason it wasn't. I thought he would grow and that I could help him grow. I was totally wrong, of course.

One thing I can encourage you to do is pay attention to red flags and run far away or you will find yourself caught up in stuff you can't get out of.

Back to the haunting question I received during my entire pregnancy: "What would you do if I died?"

My answer to that was that I'd continue to live and seek God for understanding, wisdom, peace, love, and joy. I never accepted this reality going through my pregnancy. When the doctors talked about my baby dying before I delivered, I spoke against that. I told them it was possible my baby could be healed before delivery. I believe in a God who heals, so I did not believe the doctors had the last word. I wanted God to finish the work He already started. I did not want to take the life away from my baby based on my situation.

I did not know what God was up to, so I continued to pray for healing and miracles for Royalty. I told everyone to be careful of the words they spoke, for I'd learned that words have power. What you speak, you give life to. I never said during my pregnancy, "My baby might die." Honestly, I did not believe she would. I truly believed that God was able. Now, I did have moments where the enemy tried to attack my thoughts and had me questioning if I really believed God for a miracle. But I did believe God was able, and I continued to declare and decree life and not death over my baby.

When I went into labor with my baby girl, you'd think that would have been one of the scariest moments of my life, but it was not. Was I a little worried? Yes, because I went into labor unexpectedly and then needed a C-Section to give my baby girl every possible chance at life. The doctors said the same thing until she was born, still uncertain about her condition, how bad or how good it was. They knew a little but not much, and the little they did know, was all bad.

The happiest moment of my life was when I heard my baby cry when she came out. I will never forget that moment. God showed me once again that He is able. God showed me that man does not have the last word; He does. God showed me that He was a healer and a miracle worker. God showed me that my baby had a chance at life. God showed me that through my obedience I received my blessing. God showed me how the devil tried to tell me everything opposite of what He had planned. God showed me that no LBWC could stop what He wanted me to see, feel, and experience—which was life given to my baby. God breathed into my baby's nostrils and she was alive. I was excited and more than thankful while on the hospital bed.

Royalty was, however, born with abnormalities, some of which the doctors previously had warned us of, but the abnormalities were not as bad as they'd stated. At several appointments, the doctors had said my baby girl's heart was growing out of her chest, and they strongly urged me to get an abortion. I told them, "No, the devil is a lie," and when she was born, her heart was inside her chest and she had a heartbeat. I was so thankful to God.

When the nurse brought Royalty to me and put her on my skin, she opened her eyes, yawned, and smiled as I talked to both her and God at the same time. I began to pray and plead the blood of Jesus over my baby girl. I continued to praise God in the delivery room, and I will forever praise God for as long as I live no matter the trial or tribulation.

My baby girl was born May 9, 2016, at 4:50 p.m. Her heartbeat grew fainter, and at 6:46 p.m., the doctors said she had gone to Heaven. My baby girl was true royalty and a warrior. After the doctors said she went to be with the Lord, she continued to open one of her eyes here and there for the next few hours. Her godmother, Monique, came in the room a few minutes after 6:46 p.m., and when Royalty heard her voice, she opened one of her eyes. I will never forget that day and everything God revealed to me during and after my pregnancy.

Chapter 11

Pregnant With a Purpose

⁴ You are the light of the world. A town built on a hill cannot be hidden. ⁵ Neither do people light a lamp and put it under a bowl. Instead they put it on a stand, and it gives light to everyone in the house. ⁶ In the same way, let your light shine before others, that they may see the good deeds and glorify your Father in heaven.
[Matthew 5:14-16]

Have you ever sat back and thought about your purpose? I am sure many of you reading this have done that countless of times. I hope you know that you are put here on Earth for far greater purposes than what life appears. Sometimes I am sure you become confused and lost in the motions of your day-to-day life and activities. You may worry, and a spirit of fear sits in your mind, telling you things such as: "Life will never get better," "You may never fulfill your purpose," "God doesn't love you," and "Things will always seem so hard."

We've all had these moments where these thoughts have crept into our minds and stayed there. I have learned that as quick as those thoughts and spirits creep up on you, you must cast those thoughts down, decree victory, and declare that you will receive the promises God has over your life. You must decree and declare a peace of mind and clarity of your purpose.

God has promised us all greater. God wants us to have more than our current situation. God wants us all to live in abundance. God does not want us to be broke and live paycheck to paycheck. One thing I love about God is that he gives us freewill. We make our own decisions and choices each day. We choose to go left or right. He will give us directions and guidance, but it's up to us to follow Him. God does not make us do anything. God does not even make us believe in Him, so why would He make us listen to Him?

Let's talk about being pregnant with a purpose. God has designed us all to fulfill different assignments, purposes, and destinies. Each of us is pregnant with a purpose. The biggest test is to fulfill your purpose. The enemy's plan is to stop you from fulfilling your purpose before you die. It is essential for us to fulfill our purposes here on earth before we die.

Ask yourself how you'd feel if you died without fulfilling the purpose God created you to fulfill. How would you feel when judgment day came and God said you did not do the one thing He needed you to do most? How would you feel if you failed God?

Sometimes we look at other people and compare their lives and their purposes to our own. When we do this, it is because we are in an identity crisis. When you are unsure where you are headed, who you are, and what God has designed you to be, you are in an identity crisis. God does not want us to compare ourselves and our lives to others.

God wants you to focus on Him, trust Him, and allow Him to do the work in you.

Since we are all pregnant with purposes, it is the enemy's number one plan is to get us to abort that thang. The enemy has many different plans, tactics, and ways that are designed to knock us off track. It is through God you receive your strength to fight. God will give you strength that you never thought you had. God will fight for you even when you don't ask Him to. What if I told you that God went before you to stop plans of the enemy without you knowing? My prayer for so long has been "God protect me from the things seen and unseen."

God truly protects us from the hands and the plans of the enemy each day. I am so thankful how God created each of us in our own unique way. I am also so thankful that He created us in His own image. Genesis 1:27 states: "So God created human beings in his own image. In the image of God he created them; male and female he created them."

When I learned that God created me just like Him, I began to see Him in myself. I also rejoiced, thinking about how great, mighty, and powerful He was and knowing I was just like Him in my own unique way.

The scripture I kept close to my heart and prayed over my sweet baby Royalty throughout my pregnancy was Jeremiah 1:5: "I knew you before I formed you in your mother's womb. Before you were born I set you apart and appointed you as my prophet to the nations." This scripture has so much depth, and I dissected it to pieces.

First, I thanked God for my child and the fact that He predestined me to be a mother before I was even born. Not only did he predestine me to be a mother of one, but of two children. I thanked Him for assigning my children to me and the purposes He attached to their lives because being pregnant both times taught me so much about God, my life, and my purpose. I cried at how good God was, how His plans were better than our plans, and His thoughts better than our thoughts. I don't think I quite got the reality of His plans being better than my plans until my second pregnancy with Royalty.

Then, I thanked God for making my daughter so precious. I thought, *Wait, she's a prophet to the nations?* I was astounded by the mighty gift growing inside my womb. I didn't know how else to feel but blessed. And at the time, I didn't know her true purpose in my life.

My daughter opened up so many things inside of me that I didn't know existed. One of the greatest things she birthed out of me was the revelation of this book. Had I not been pregnant with her and gone through the journey with her, this book would not have been written.

During the process of being pregnant with her, God was healing and delivering me on a whole new level. I had not only been praying for Royalty's healing but also my own during this pregnancy. All along, God was answering my prayers and I did not know this; however, I did expect it.

Listening to God and writing this book allowed me to go through more healing and deliverance. I did not know this until God revealed it to me. I am thankful that I ultimately listened to God, began to pray more, exercised my faith daily, and became intentional about a more intimate relationship with God. All this allowed me not to fall into the hands of the enemy. I was able to overcome all the obstacles, scars, and weapons thrown at me through this journey of being pregnant with Royalty because of God.

Had I gone through with the abortion as the doctors wanted, I would have messed up the process God was taking me through, which would have ultimately messed up the birth of this book. I would not have been in the right place to write the book. I am so glad I listened to the Holy Spirit and continued with my pregnancy.

As I said at the beginning of this book, years previously God revealed to me that one day I would be an author of books. I tried time and time again to begin writing, but a book never materialized. I later learned that the time hadn't been right. One thing God revealed to me going through this season: "If it's the right time that I have predestined something for you, then it will happen. If it is not the right time, I won't allow it to happen."

I have gotten to the place where I am living in God's will for my life and not my own. I have completely submitted to Him, His ways, and His thoughts and have allowed Him to have control. With that being said, the book would not have been written any other time because it was not the time God predestined. In the seasons when I tried to execute the vision God gave me about becoming a writer, he said, "There are things you have not been through yet that I still need you to experience before you write this book." I answered, "Okay," not knowing what it would be or what to expect. To be honest, I never thought it would be to receive a fatal diagnosis while pregnant.

I also never thought this pregnancy would bring me closer to God and that my purpose would be more visible through this test. I now see clearly exactly what God wants and wanted me to see all along. I have been pregnant with a purpose before he formed me in my mother's womb, but I did not realize what I was carrying until recently. The scripture Jeremiah 1:5 describes who I am and who you are as well. God created us to be a prophet to all the nations.

God sent Jesus to be a prophet to all the nations when He was here in the flesh. Remember, God created us all in His image. I have the same strengths and power as you do. God created us all to have a journey, a story, and a testimony to share to nations while giving Him the glory. God created us all to be able to prophesy to people. I have no greater ability than you do.

The only questions are:

- Are you tired of living the way you want to live?
- Do you believe in God?
- Do you believe in the God that's in you?
- Do you believe God is for you?
- Do you believe you have a purpose?
- Do you trust God?
- Do you trust God enough to walk in blind faith?
- Will you surrender to God?
- Will you submit to God?
- Do you want God to change you?

- Do you want to live the life God has planned for you?

- Do you want the promises of God?

- Do you want to be healed?

- Do you want to be delivered?

- Are you willing to get uncomfortable to get comfortable?

- Are you willing to be stretched?

- Are you willing to be in the wilderness?

- Are you ready for God to do a work in you?

- Are you ready for God to give you a new heart?

- Are you ready for God to use you?

Answer these questions. If your answers are all YES, then you are ready for the process of healing and deliverance. You are ready for God to do things in you and through you that you have never imagined. God will use you in small and mighty ways. In your eyes it may be small, but in God's eyes it may be mighty.

Two of the best decisions I made in life were submitting and surrendering to God wholeheartedly. When you do this, you must trust God and allow Him to lead and direct you everywhere. When God tells you to do something even when you don't understand it, just do it. The best thing is to be obedient. The Bible says obedience is greater than sacrifice.

In 1 Samuel 15:22: "But Samuel replied, 'What is more pleasing to the LORD: your burnt offerings and sacrifices or your obedience to his voice? Listen! Obedience is better than sacrifice, and submission is better than offering the fat of rams.'"

Always remember that obedience is better than sacrifice. Trust in the Lord even when you don't understand. I had to trust God while being pregnant after I was given such a fatal diagnosis. I had to trust God when I was writing this book even when I was tired and did not understand why He wanted me to be so transparent. In these very tests, I had to exercise my faith and walk blindly knowing God was with me, by my side, in me, and had plans to use me. Just like the scripture Romans 8:31 states, "What shall we then say to these things? If God *be* for us, who *can be* against us?"

I rejoice and find my strength knowing that God gave me the visions, the tests, the trials, the obstacles, the scars, and the journey—all for my good. I rejoice knowing that God will fulfill all the promises He gave to me. I rejoice knowing that my God is bigger than the devil and any demons that try to attack me. I rejoice knowing God is my everything. I rejoice knowing I have tried God for myself, so I know what the Bible says and the testimonies I've heard all my life are true.

I rejoice knowing I am still here on Earth and still have a chance to fulfill my purpose. I rejoice knowing God loves me, forgives me, and has not given up on me even when I have given up on myself. I rejoice knowing things will get better. I rejoice knowing the best is yet to come. I rejoice knowing the enemy is only after me because the testimony that I have yet to develop is so powerful it will change many lives, so he wants to kill, steal, and destroy it before it is even manifested. I rejoice knowing I am pregnant with a purpose and that God wants me to share it with the world. God also wants you to share what He has put in your womb too. God put you here to change nations just like me.

The scriptures that God has blessed me with after the birth of my baby girl, Royalty, who brings me so much wisdom, revelation, and confirmation, are:

Ecclesiastes 7: 1-29 NIV
Wisdom

"[1] A good name is better than fine perfume,

and the day of death better than the day of birth.

[2] It is better to go to a house of mourning

than to go to a house of feasting,

for death is the destiny of everyone;

the living should take this to heart.

[3] Frustration is better than laughter,

because a sad face is good for the heart.

[4] The heart of the wise is in the house of mourning,

but the heart of fools is in the house of pleasure.

[5] It is better to heed the rebuke of a wise person

than to listen to the song of fools.

[6] Like the crackling of thorns under the pot,

so is the laughter of fools.

This too is meaningless.

[7] Extortion turns a wise person into a fool,

and a bribe corrupts the heart.

[8] The end of a matter is better than its beginning,

and patience is better than pride.

[9] Do not be quickly provoked in your spirit,

for anger resides in the lap of fools.

[10] Do not say, "Why were the old days better than these?"

For it is not wise to ask such questions.

[11] Wisdom, like an inheritance, is a good thing

and benefits those who see the sun.

[12] Wisdom is a shelter

as money is a shelter,

but the advantage of knowledge is this:

Wisdom preserves those who have it.

[13] Consider what God has done:

Who can straighten

what he has made crooked?

[14] When times are good, be happy;

but when times are bad, consider this:

God has made the one

as well as the other.

Therefore, no one can discover

anything about their future.

[15] In this meaningless life of mine I have seen both of these:

the righteous perishing in their righteousness,

and the wicked living long in their wickedness.

[16] Do not be overrighteous,

neither be overwise—

why destroy yourself?
¹⁷ Do not be overwicked,

and do not be a fool—

why die before your time?
¹⁸ It is good to grasp the one

and not let go of the other.

Whoever fears God will avoid all extremes.
¹⁹ Wisdom makes one wise person more powerful

than ten rulers in a city.
²⁰ Indeed, there is no one on earth who is righteous,

no one who does what is right and never sins.
²¹ Do not pay attention to every word people say,

or you may hear your servant cursing you—
²² for you know in your heart

that many times you yourself have cursed others.
²³ All this I tested by wisdom and I said,

"I am determined to be wise"—

but this was beyond me.
²⁴ Whatever exists is far off and most profound—

who can discover it?
²⁵ So I turned my mind to understand,

to investigate and to search out wisdom and the scheme of

things

and to understand the stupidity of wickedness

and the madness of folly.

[26] I find more bitter than death

 the woman who is a snare,

whose heart is a trap

 and whose hands are chains.

The man who pleases God will escape her,

 but the sinner she will ensnare.

[27] "Look," says the Teacher, "this is what I have discovered:

"Adding one thing to another to discover the scheme of things—

[28] while I was still searching

 but not finding—

I found one upright man among a thousand,

 but not one upright woman among them all.

[29] This only have I found:

 God created mankind upright,

 but they have gone in search of many schemes."

Chapter 12

Deliverance is Real

When you get to the point where you want change and want to do things God's way, this is where the process of healing and deliverance can take place. You have to begin to speak differently. Tell God, "I submit to you, Lord. I surrender my all to you. I want to be more like you. Heal me. Change me. Deliver me from all the evil."

God will begin to work in you and around you. God will change your mindset, your habits, your old ways, and your relationships. God will remove things and people from your life that should not be there. God will give you wisdom and discernment on a whole new level. While in this process, the important part is not to run away from God. Yes, you will be uncomfortable because your life is changing right before your eyes. Do not run back to Satan's traps and tactics.

It is so easy for God to change us. God can remove things and people immediately, but He wants to take you through a process. Have you heard the phrase "Anything worth having is hard to get"? So, just know this process is not easy but is worth every scar, trial, test, obstacle, and blessings to come.

As I went through the process of healing and deliverance, my language changed. Also, my mind, thoughts, and actions changed. My words and the people around me changed. Everything about me began to change. I did not have complete control over my life as I thought I had. I didn't have control over my then-current situation, which was the diagnosis during my pregnancy.

God started to do so much work with me, and it got to a point where I submitted to Him completely. God revealed so many things to me about myself. Some of these things about which I had no idea hindered me from walking in my purpose. God showed me people in my circle who would not and could not walk into this next season with me. Some of them I didn't want to accept giving up at the time. I was too comfortable and content in the relationships that I was not aware of the dead weight they caused in my life. I know you are thinking it is not easy to let go of people, places, and things you may be comfortable with, but it is a must in order for God to heal and deliver you.

God wants to make all things new and be the God of restoration. God wants to be the God of healing and deliverance. The question is, are you ready to be made whole? Are you ready to be made new? Are you ready to be the curse breaker for your generation? Are you ready to be healed? Are you ready to be delivered? Are you ready to be very uncomfortable? Are you ready to experience God on a new level? Are you ready to see the power of God like never before? Are you ready to submit and surrender to God? Are you ready to dig deep into your soul and your past to see what curses have been assigned to you and your family? Are you ready to be exposed to what is hindering you? Are you ready for generational curses to be broken? Are you ready for bondage and strongholds to be released from your life? Are you ready to walk in your fullness and allow the light of God to shine brightly from you?

If your answer is yes to all those questions, you are ready for the process God is readying to take you through. In this season, you have to be fully equipped with the Armor of God that I told you about. Your prayer life must increase. Your worship must increase. Your studying of the Bible must increase, and your time spent with God must increase.

The beginning stages of my healing and deliverance were very uncomfortable. Right away, God shook things up, causing so much havoc in my life. Yes, this was God. God is a jealous God, and a God that will curse you for being disobedient. At the time, I was disobedient and living a life of idolatry, meaning I had idols in my life that I worshipped and/or put in front of God. I did not fully see and/or believe this once it was revealed to me. I wanted to think that God was the head of my life and I put Him first. However, truly the life I was living did not reflect that.

As God gave me wisdom going through this process, He revealed some of my ways, thoughts, actions, and sins that I needed to change. I saw myself from a different angle going through this process. Talk about being shaken up, woken up, and eyes cleared up during this time. I was truly sleeping on the truth, meaning I was living a lie. I made up in my mind who I was. I dressed how I wanted people to see me. I talked how I wanted people to hear me. I presented myself everywhere I went to be a different person than who I truly was deep down.

I had reached a point where I was broken emotionally, financially, mentally, physically, and spiritually. In every aspect of my life, I was broken. My life was literally in pieces. God showed me I was torn on the inside but appeared whole on the outside. I was afraid on the inside but fearless on the outside. I was lost on the inside but had a sense of direction on the outside. I was ugly on the inside but beautiful on the outside. God revealed to me that I was all jacked up—if you get the picture.

Most of you reading this are at this point or have been recently. This is a scary place to be in. You literally are a mess in full circle. Yes, you may know God and have a relationship with Him and still be a mess like this. Yes, you may have been baptized, filled with the Holy Spirit, saved, sanctified, attend church every Sunday, and may even be involved in ministry. This still does not cover up the mess you are on the inside.

You may not see the complete mess you are, but if you see a little bit, you are good. When you are able to see your brokenness, you should want to be changed. You should want God to change you. A portion of my cry out to God sounded like this:

"Lord, please save me. Heal me, God. I want to be made new. Lord, take everything away that I don't need. Shut every door in my life that needs to be shut. I just want you. I am yours. I see that I am a mess. My heart is heavy. My mind is full and racing. I am lost. I don't know which way to go. I am tired of dressing everything up to look good on the outside when I am dying on the inside. God, change me. Change my mind, my thoughts, my actions. I want to be just like you. I know you have called me to be greater and to do mighty things. I see that. I have been so busy trying to figure things out, set things up, and accomplish so much I did not see what I was doing wrong. I did not realize I was trying to control my life full circle. I now see that. I surrender to you, God. I give myself to you, God. I want you to use me. Lead me, God. Guide me. Take me places you want me to go. When I speak, I want people to hear you. When people see me, I want them to see you. God, I want to be in your presence. God, I realize I don't want to live the life I have been living. God, I want to receive all the things you have promised me. God, I know you are able. God, I submit to your will and your ways. I give everything to you. Take me. I am yours. Heal me, God. Deliver me. Lord, keep confirming my purpose to me and give me clarity if I do not truly know what it is. Change my heart, my mind, my thoughts, and my ways. I love you, Lord, and I believe you are able. Amen."

I literally cried out daily to God. My posture changed when I sought Him. I was never used to bowing, on my knees praying. I mean, I have done that here and there in my lifetime, but it was not a normal thing for me. Well, this became a normal thing for me. I even found a secret place in my house that I made for me and God. It was my walk in the closet at the time, and I made it into my prayer closet.

Rewinding back some years to the first time in my life that I actually cried out and prayed to God for healing and deliverance, I was in college. This was directly after my diagnosis of Lupus and Fibromyalgia. God began to do the work in me then, but I ran from the process. I stopped the process. I encourage you to stay the course, so you can get the promises of God and walk in your calling in God's timing and not your own. I know God allowed me to run because He is a God who can do anything, so He could have easily stopped me and brought me back to the process sooner. However, God knows us better than we know ourselves, so He allows us to walk roads, run places, and seek things from people and places so we can run back to Him.

God wants us to genuinely and sincerely seek Him. He does not want it to be forced. He is a God who gives us the power of freewill. We can make choices of our own and do things of our own. However, He is a God who will show you how powerful He is and how He created you for a purpose.

When I found out I was pregnant, everything in my life fell apart. It was not because I was intentionally doing it; it was God intentionally doing it. God is intentional and never failing. God literally started to remove things and people from my life. God closed doors and took me from places where I was comfortable. I was not happy in these places, but I was comfortable. That is a sad place to be: not happy but comfortable. This is the place where most people reside.

Let me speak on that for a moment. You are not happy, but you are comfortable. I cannot reiterate enough; this is a sad place to be. Most of the times in life, we are in this place—not happy but comfortable. Why stay in this place? If you know there is better, why stay in a place of hurt, confusion, anger, frustration, and misery? Some of you are choosing to be in these very places but turn around and blame God for where you are. You should be praising God for all He does and the fact that He has given you clarity that you are not happy but comfortable.

You have to know those thoughts did not come from you. That was the Holy Spirit speaking. God has promised us all a better life through Him. God has promised us all different things, and He wants to fulfill them all. You have to put yourself in the position to believe and receive them. You know how the Bible says "Faith without works is dead"? There are things you need to do in order for God to do the rest. God is waiting on you to make the first move out of faith and to make the next few moves out of your obedience. The Bible says "Obedience is better than sacrifice."

It is better to listen to God and obey His commands than sacrifice some things. God loves when we are obedient to Him. In the Bible, the Book of Deuteronomy talks about how God blesses us for being obedient and curses us for being disobedient. The Book of Deuteronomy is a great book to read, and I highly suggest you read it in full while going through this process of deliverance. Also, read the books of Job and Matthew, Mark, Luke, John, Ecclesiastes, Genesis, Psalms, Proverbs, and Revelation.

All these books have blessed me in ways you cannot imagine. My faith and foundation with God has forever changed from the reading of these books. Other books have blessed me, but going through the process of healing and deliverance these are very significant to me.

Let's dig a little deeper in regards to curses, demons, bondages, hindrances, and soul ties. Sometimes when God is changing you on the inside, you're not even aware of it. Certain things you must be aware of so you can call it out and speak directly to it. When it comes down to demons attacking you, you have to know what is attacking you. This requires a few things such as knowing the Word of God, having a relationship with God, hearing from God, having a body of warriors in Christ around you, and/or be a part of a church, preferably a deliverance ministry.

It is important to be part of a church that teaches the Word from the Bible and that you're learning something. However, I believe being a part of a deliverance ministry during your deliverance process is important for so many reasons. Mainly, because they teach, discuss, and focus on what demons are assigned to you and how to get rid of them. They teach you how to identify the demons and how to cast them out of you and others. Deliverance ministry focuses on getting to the root of all the bondage, strongholds, curses, spirits, and so many other things that have you in the place that you are now.

During the deliverance process, you must identify what demons are assigned to you and attacking you. These are some of the demons I have identified that have attacked me:

The spirit of sickness and disease, the spirit of fornication, the spirit of guilt, the spirit of shame, the spirit of self-regret, the spirit of hate, the spirit of self-hatred, the spirit of abuse, the spirit of neglect, the spirit of insecurity, the spirit of anger, the spirit of resentment, the spirit of worry, the spirit of fear, the spirit of anxiety, the spirit of depression, the spirit of gossip, the spirit of rejection, the spirit of abortion, spirit of indecisiveness, spirit of double-mindedness, the religious spirit, and the spirit of identity.

There are so many spirits assigned and attached to each of us by Satan. Most people are unaware of these demonic spirits attacking them and controlling them. The spirits need a willing body in which to fulfill their assignments. If you are unaware how the demons come dressed and casted, you will continue to give them authority to use you and operate in you. The study of demons is real, especially during the process of deliverance—not just studying them but identifying them, casting them out daily, and not allowing them to capture your mind, thoughts, actions, and body.

These spirits want to kill, steal, and destroy your mind, thoughts, action, purpose, dreams, assignments, gifts, talents, abilities, and most importantly, your relationship with God. Our hearts, minds, and thoughts have all been misconstrued by this cruel world and the demonic spirits that are in it. Do not let Satan win. You have the victory in Jesus.

Once you begin this process of deliverance, do not run from it. This process is not comfortable, but there is so much inner work for God to do. Before God can allow you to fulfill your promise, you have to acknowledge your heart's condition and let God change you. God has to empty you of the mess that's been put in you.

When you walk through this process with God, the devil is mad because you have strayed away from him. Always remember: Because you are pregnant with a purpose, the devil will try to get you to abort what God has given you. You have to protect it and not give Satan authority to reign in your body, mind, thoughts, and actions.

Declare and decree healing and deliverance over your life. You must speak to the devil daily and say:

"I am a curse breaker. The Lord has caused me to be the breaker of a curse of my generation. I declare and decree healing and deliverance over my mind, body, and spirit. I call healing and deliverance into my life. I declare and decree that the spirit of sickness, anger, anxiety, worry, doubt, neglect, abuse, and rejection flee right now in the name of Jesus. In the name of Jesus, you must flee. Go far, far away, and never come back. I call healing over my life. I call the spirit of joy, peace, love, self-control, clarity, discernment, understanding, and wisdom into my life. Satan, you have no way here. You must flee at the name of Jesus. Get back Satan. Amen"

When you talk to God, you must confess:

"God, I love you, and I thank you for healing and deliverance. I thank you for saving me. I thank you for loving me. I thank you for never giving up on me. I thank you for the work that you are doing in me. You are my God and my God alone. You are seated far above every power and authority. God, I believe in you. I look to you and call on you for healing. God, I have seen you do it before, so I know you can do it again. Have your way in my life. I am nothing without you. I have tried it on my own, and I cannot live my life without you. Have your way, God. Heal me, God. Heal my family in Jesus name, Amen."

Remember the scripture that says "I can do all things through Christ who strengthens me"? God has given you the power to break every curse over your life. The demon that tried to destroy a generational relationship with God will not control you. God is calling you to a new life in Him that is filled with praise, adoration, and power. God will reveal to you the power of Him and the sovereignty of Him. I declare that your walk will reveal a new sound and a new light of God. God is calling you to a place where you want more. God is going to fill you with Heaven's best to get you to the next place.

I pray that you surrender and submit to God. Trust Him in all His ways. Stay the process. Do not run away from God. Running away and being impatient just takes you back to square one again. Be patient and have faith. This is a blind faith walk. You must walk with your head held high, trusting God, and not knowing one step from the next. During this time, God will reveal to you the greatest weapon He has given you. He will also reveal and confirm your purpose. I know my weapon and my purpose. I pray this book has helped you with your relationship with God and has given you a deeper look into the life of a believer who has struggled in her walk and obedience in Christ.

We are not perfect and never will be, so stop trying to be. I have to remind myself of this daily. During my deliverance process, God revealed to me that He wanted me to write this book. This is the first of many books. God instructed me to be transparent and authentic in this book because there are men and women who sit wearing the same or similar shoes. There is nothing to be ashamed about. God also later revealed to me that this was a part of my deliverance process. Let God do the work in you that needs to be done so that you can get all the promises He has for you. I highly encourage you to get a notebook and journal through your deliverance and healing process. Writing is very therapeutic for me, so I encourage others to write as well.

Remember, deliverance is real. It is necessary to being whole. It is essential to go through to walk fully in your purpose and it will happen. Give God your Yes and trust the process. You will be delivered.

Chapter 13

Revelations

Walking with God is amazing. Putting God first is amazing. Surrendering to God is even better. Submitting to God is challenging. Trusting God is challenging. But all of them together are God's will for your life, so the outcome is far greater than you can imagine. When I submitted to God and surrendered to Him and His will for my life, things began to shake up in my life. Life was not what I was used to. Life became different, and my tests grew larger and harder. My wisdom and knowledge increased as well. My vision and hearing changed. Nothing was the same anymore.

I am not saying this to scare you but to warn you. God sends warnings before destruction.

Swimming in the Pool—Faith and Trusting God.

One day I planned to go to the gym to work out and swim. At the time, I didn't own a swimming suit, so I went to the store closest to the gym and purchased a suit. I was determined to swim this particular day and wouldn't let the thought slip my mind. After I completed my daily workout, I went to the pool. All three lanes had one person in each.

This did not stop my urge to swim because I immediately remembered orientation, where they said two people could be in each lane. The water was cold, so I entered slowly. I thought, *Maybe I should get in the hot tub instead. This water is colder than I thought it would be,* but I kept going. When I entered the first lane, I asked the man in the lane, "Do you mind if we share this lane?" He replied, "I'm about to leave anyway, so go right ahead." I dipped in and out of the water. At the same time, I talked to God.

After my first two laps, I realized the other two men in the pool were swimming backwards. My first thought was, *I should swim backwards too.* Then I realized, though I had learned to swim at a young age, I hadn't learned to swim backwards. I've tried to swim backwards all my life but never felt as though I completely accomplished it. I would lose my balance and my back would arch and my face would go underwater. I understood the concept, but maybe I hadn't practiced it enough to be good at it.

As I approached the front of the pool, God allowed me to see a blue floaty, an aid to help individuals float above water. I remembered them from when I was a child, but I had never used them much. In that moment, God spoke to me, told me to grab the floaty, and put it behind my back. I did as he said, leaned back, and treaded water with my hands and feet. At some point, I closed my eyes and gave God thanks.

While treading, I moved down the lane of the swimming pool to the ᴠosite end, which was the goal. At one point, I bumped into the ᴠ I had to stop and reposition myself. As I did so, I was moving

110

without treading. God immediately spoke to me: "Look at me moving you without you doing anything." Smiling in amazement, I thanked Him repeatedly.

I returned to treading water, which allowed me to move a little faster. Then the man in the lane next to me quickly swam forward, splashing water from his lane onto my face. I wiped my eyes so I could see clearly. God told me, "People will try to come to distract you from your purpose, but I need you to wipe your eyes so that you can see, move around, and keep going." I treaded water again, listening to the voice of God. As I neared the opposite end of the pool, waves struck me so hard I could not move. I kept treading, harder and harder, because my goal was to make it to the end of the pool.

God talked to me again, saying, "Stop moving. Trust me. I am allowing you not to go anywhere even though you think you have the strength and ability to do so. You do not. You do not have any control over where you go. Sometimes I have to stop you and sit you still for a moment because I have to get you back together. You may get off course, become distracted, become comfortable, become too excited. You may think you are moving yourself and think you need your own strength, so I have to remind you that I, alone, am the reason why you move and why you accomplish things. Sometimes I have to allow you to think you are accomplishing things so I can wake you and show you that you cannot do anything without me."

God continued: "I can take you far. I can take you to places you have never seen if you just trust me. Do you trust me? Do you trust me like you say you do? If so, why do you feel it is you who can get you to the end of the pool and back? Why is it that you picked today to swim? Why do you forget about me some days? Why do you trust me in some situations but not all? Why, when something seems so hard, do you want to give up? Why, when I stop you or detour you, do you think I am punishing you or that I'm not with you? Why do you despise the process I take you through? Why do you want to rush the process I am putting you through?"

As God talked to me and asked me questions, I floated to the other side of the pool. I also told God, "I trust you. I trust you, Lord. I trust you. I am sorry for times when I have underestimated you. I am sorry for the times when I thought I was in control of my life and my destiny. I am sorry for allowing people and things to distract me and knock me off course because I put my trust in them. I am sorry I give up on you too easily. I am sorry, Lord, for not trusting you like I say I do. I do trust you, Lord, but I struggle at times. Lord, I trust you but help my unbelief."

I was amazed what God was telling me. I rejoiced, glad I listened to my Holy Spirit to buy a swimsuit and swim that day after my workout. I thanked God for loving me no matter what. Even when I mess up and don't trust God or move away and run from my calling, he still loves me. God still finds a way to reach and talk to me. God finds a way to teach me things and to shower the love on me. God finds a way to send me instructions, confirmation, and revelation. I am always astounded about my God and what He is capable of.

In that moment, God revealed two significant things He has been teaching me all my life that I am sure you can relate to:

1. You have no control over ANYTHING; and

2. Trust me in ALL YOUR WAYS, THOUGHTS, and ACTIONS.

Another revelation God recently gave me and continues to remind me about is patience.

While driving my car one day, I was speeding to my destination. Traffic and construction slowed me down. When I was finally able to pick up speed, a car passed me, got in front of me, and drove too slowly. I was immediately upset.

It didn't hit me until later that God used that moment to speak to me. God said, "SLOW DOWN." I was moving too fast and not really going anywhere. I looked around, and the cars I thought I had driven away from were all around me. The Holy Spirit said, "You are not going as fast as you think you are. Remember, I am the way and the only way. I can speed you up or slow you down. Sometimes I have to slow you down so you won't get off track or so you can get back on track."

God added, "Even when you don't see me or hear me, I am there. I have designed roadblocks, closed doors, and said no to you—all for your own good. I am God, and I am always with you. I work on things for you and around you even when you are not focused on me. Remember, slow down. You cannot get to the goal, dream, vision, gift, and/or promises faster than I designed for you. Remember that your life is predestined. I know your beginning and end before you do. I have designed everything to happen accordingly. Just trust me and follow me and you can receive all the riches and glory. I will keep reminding you to slow down because, for some reason, you still think you have control, and you have no control over your life. I run this. Slow down, be still, and be patient. You don't always have to be doing something. Let me do my work. Just sit back, watch, and give me the glory."

I pray these two revelations help you just as much as they helped me. God talks to us, but we have to be willing to listen and hear Him. If you feel you are not hearing from God, ask God to give you a double portion of the Holy Spirit. Tell God you want to hear from Him and know that it is Him.

What I have learned is that most of us overthink when God talks to us. We think the moment should be magical, but God has many ways of talking to each of us. God knows you, and He knows how to get to you, so He has his secret ways of talking to you. Seek Him and you shall find Him. Knock and the door shall open. When God talks to you and gives you instructions, be obedient to Him. Don't get deliverance twisted. Some people think when God heals and delivers you that you don't face the same issues or demons again. Deliverance is a daily walk for the rest of your life. It does not happen overnight and then— boom!—no more attacks, no more praying, no more fasting. That is a lie. Deliverance is daily for the rest of your life.

Keep seeking God, deliverance, and healing. Stay in the process, keep your mind on Jesus, trust God, and enjoy the process. Deliverance is a beautiful thing. The more deliverance I receive, the more excited I become. I am still been healed and delivered daily.

Chapter 14

A Letter to Royalty

When I found out I was having you, I was extremely happy and knew you were destined for greatness. All I could think about was how blessed I was to be your mother. Before I knew your gender, God told me to name you Royalty. I looked up the meaning of Royalty, and it was biblical and sacramental. God confirmed to me through the meaning of your name what your purpose was. Royalty has many meanings, but most importantly it means "powerful," "sovereign," and "a queen."

Sarai means "princess." Some that studied the Bible suggest that Sarai may signify "contentious." Contentious means causing or likely to cause an argument; controversial.

Your purpose definitely caused controversy throughout the course of the thirty-four weeks and five days you were here. I was not at all mad about the controversy because you and God blessed me with grace to walk through it all with my head held high. Though some days were extremely hard, I would never think to give up on you. Some may not get why I held on so long and strong, but it is not for everyone to understand. The only answer I have is "God." Jesus did it.

Your name Royalty Sarai signifies the gracious purposes and promises of God. This biblical name became a sign and seal of an established covenant between God, you, and me.

The moment I found out your diagnosis of Limb Body Wall Complex, I was highly encouraged by specialists to abort you. I knew then you were even more special than I had ever imagined. Through this journey, God kept whispering to me, reminding me that He was right by my side and that He was the same God today as He was yesterday.

God kept reminding me of your name and how powerful you were. God continued to remind me that he created you in His image and I would not be upset at the end of my pregnancy. God informed me that when you're pregnant with a purpose and you're marked for greatness, the enemy will try to continuously attack you in every way. Anytime purpose is trying to be fulfilled, there is resistance.

I knew from the beginning God did not make you sick because sickness is not of God. It is from the devil. I knew the devil would be defeated and we would have victory in the end.

I prayed daily for miracles and a supernatural healing over your body. I pleaded the blood of Jesus, studied the Word, worshipped, praised, and prayed to God unceasingly. I did everything God instructed me to do. I prayed that God's will would be done through it all, and that's exactly what took place.

I've learned so much from you, and I thank you for all the times we had together. I thank you for molding me to be a stronger woman and to walk into my purpose. I thank you for loving me when no one else did. I thank you for continuing to remind me how great God is and how powerful I am with God. I thank you for allowing God to use you here on earth for such a short time. You fought and fought hard just like your mommy.

I love you, Royalty. I can't wait to be in Heaven with you very soon and see your beautiful face again. Tell your brother I said hi. I love and miss him. Keep watching over Mommy. I know this journey with you has just begun even though it seems like it ended here on Earth. I know something so much greater is coming from all of this.

Baby, all I want you to do is rest in peace, in Heaven, with our King and Father.

Love Always,
Mommy

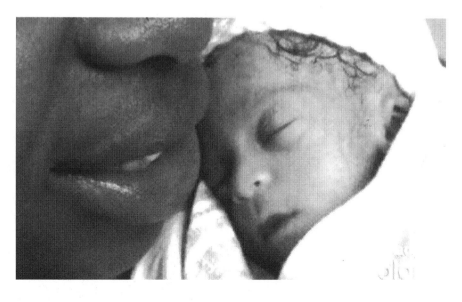

Chapter 15

A Letter to My Mommy

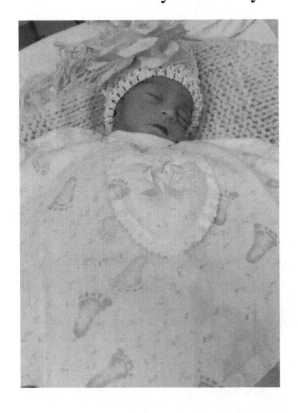

Some say that it takes forty weeks to grow a baby, but I say it took thirty four weeks to grow a Princess.

So extraordinary in every way; from the top of my head down to the soles of my feet.

Mommy, you grew me so perfectly.

While you warmed my body, I warmed your heart.

When everyone counted me out, you believed in me right from the start.

I was gifted to you from God, so uniquely special, and set apart from the rest.

The Father knew that choosing you as my Mommy would be for the very best.

A special gift housed in your womb, and most will never understand.

It was a long, and sometimes lonely road, but God had a perfect plan.

He used me as a gift to exercise your faith.

Although our encounter seemed to be brief, the lesson learned will never be erased.

The Bible says, "Faith comes by hearing and hearing by God."

I entered the world wailing as a symbol of your faith in God.

For that I want to thank you, Mommy, and even though I didn't stay.

To be absent from the body is to be present with the Lord and that means that I will never stray.

You confirmed your own prophecy.

That's why you named me Royalty, because God knew I was fit for a Queen.

I only came as a messenger to remind you of who God perceives you to be.

Keep your head held high, and even in times when your head is low, look at your Mommy scar and continue to allow your faith to grow.

On the days that you miss me, get into God's prayer and when you are in His presence I promise to meet you there.

Love,
Your angel, Royalty Sarai Jones
(By Felicia Lowery Fewell, 2016)

.

About the Author

Taneisha L. Naylor is a young Christian woman who was created by God to educate, empower, encourage, equip, and lead men and women to God. She has been walking in her ministry since she was born but did not realize that until 2011. Her life is her ministry, meaning everywhere God sends her and everyone God connects her to she walks in her God-given purpose.

She is the founder of a non-profit organization, Scars Christ Allowed to Rescue Someone, Inc. (S.C.A.R.S.). Taneisha's desire is to travel to all nations to share her testimony, share the gospel, and to bring healing and deliverance to all of God's people.

Taneisha is currently a counselor. She graduated from Northern Illinois University with a bachelor's degree in Family Consumer Nutrition Studies with an emphasis in Family Social Services and a minor in Black Studies.

Contact Taneisha at:
taneishanaylor25@gmail.com

Made in the USA
San Bernardino, CA
02 February 2017